Seeking
Our
Eden

Seeking
Our
Eden

The Dreams and Migrations
of Sarah Jameson Craig

<small>JOANNE FINDON</small>

McGill-Queen's University Press

Montreal & Kingston | London | Ithaca

© McGill-Queen's University Press 2015

ISBN 978-0-7735-4480-2 (cloth)
ISBN 978-0-7735-8185-2 (ePDF)
ISBN 978-0-7735-8186-9 (ePUB)

Legal deposit first quarter 2015
Bibliothèque nationale du Québec

Printed in Canada on acid-free paper that is 100% ancient forest free
(100% post-consumer recycled), processed chlorine free

McGill-Queen's University Press acknowledges the support of the
Canada Council for the Arts for our publishing program. We also
acknowledge the financial support of the Government of Canada
through the Canada Book Fund for our publishing activities.

Library and Archives Canada Cataloguing in Publication

Findon, Joanne, 1957–, author
Seeking our eden : the dreams and migrations of Sarah Jameson Craig
/ Joanne Findon.

Includes bibliographical references and index.
Issued in print and electronic formats.
ISBN 978-0-7735-4480-2 (bound).–ISBN 978-0-7735-8185-2 (ePDF).
–ISBN 978-0-7735-8186-9 (ePUB)

1. Craig, Sarah Jameson, 1840–1919. 2. Feminists – Canada – Biography.
3. Authors, Canadian (English) – 19th century – Biography. I. Title.

HQ1455.C73F55 2015   305.42092   C2014-906332-6
                                               C2014-906333-4

For Sarah, who was ahead of her time,

and for Tamsyn, the Girl of the Future

Contents

Illustrations

Acknowledgments

This project has taken more than two decades to come to fruition, and many people have helped along the way. At the Charlotte County Archives in St Andrews, New Brunswick, two wonderful archivists assisted me: first, Charlotte McAdam and then, more recently, Janice Fairney. Their generous help has been invaluable. Thanks also to Shirley O'Neill, archives volunteer extraordinaire, who kept in touch with me about the project through many years and sent me regular updates, most notably when the descendants of one of Sarah and Joel Craig's original colony-scheme contacts turned up with copies of the Universal Progressive Reform Association pledges from the early 1860s. I also thank the many librarians who have helped me to find copies of books such as *The Hydropathic Encyclopedia* and journals such as the *Herald of Health* in archives and university libraries.

I am extremely grateful, as well, for the financial support that this project has received. I wish to thank the Symons Trust Fund for Canadian Studies at Trent University and Senator Nancy Ruth for their generous support of the publication of this book. Thanks are also due to York University for awarding me an ORA Major Research Grant in 1996–97, which funded the first stages of my research, and to the *Beaver* (now *Canada's History*) for publishing an early article about the colony scheme. And I am grateful to the anonymous readers who read this manuscript twice and whose insightful comments and helpful suggestions have made it a much better book than it would have been without their advice. Several friends and colleagues have read portions of the manuscript over the years; special thanks go to Steve Riddle, Margaret Steffler, Suzanne Bailey, Michael Peterman, and James Neufeld, who have all encouraged me to press on with this project, and to Doreen Sherlaw, who provided key information about the Craig and Blenkarn families. At McGill-Queen's University Press I am extremely grateful to Mark Abley for his insight and gracious advice and to Jessica Howarth and Helen Hajnoczky for all their generous assistance.

Finally, I pay tribute to Sarah Jameson Craig herself for her lifelong commitment to women's equality and for leaving such eloquent written records of her lived experience. She always wanted her voice to be heard; now, almost a century after her death, it finally will be.

Seeking
Our
Eden

Introduction

Sometime in the winter of 1853–54 a New Brunswick teenager ran away from home. Such behaviour is not unusual today, but in the 1850s few Canadian girls of fourteen dared to travel far from home alone; fewer still were driven by the dreams that propelled Sarah Jameson from her humble cabin in the New Brunswick bush and onto the road to St Andrews. But Sarah was no ordinary Canadian girl: Sarah wanted to be a writer. And so years later she described her daring adventure, using her storytelling skills to craft a brief narrative that has tension, a climax, and a resolution:

> I hatched a plan, all by myself, so senseless and preposterous, that I often wonder how such a crazy thought ever had place in my brain. I had a notion that father and mother were too strict with us, and especially hard and severe with me. I, being the only girl then able to help mother with the heavy work, had to take my share of it. I hated work, and would gladly have spent most of my time in playing, reading, writing, and roaming the fields and woods; dreaming of great things I would do in the distant future. Some of the reading that came in my way had a pernicious effect on my mind,

giving me altogether false views of life. I read of more than
one young person who had run away from too arbitrary rule
at home, made their way among strangers, succeeded in their
chosen path, won big laurels, and came home to surprise
their friends by some sudden, theatrical appearance in their
midst … and be crowned with honor and admiration! And
I verily believed that I, a girl of fourteen, could travel alone,
airily and safely in this idealized path and achieve and win,
as my heroes had done. I knew I should want money; but
I imagined I had only to ask some of father's friends in St
Andrews for a few hundreds in his name, to receive it!
(Memoir, 26)

Sarah goes on to recount how she actually did start for St
Andrews, having obtained her mother's permission to attend a
church prayer meeting in the next village; but instead she took a
different path: "I crossed Bonney Brook, as I imagined, for the last
time in years; called at Aunt Martha's at Clarence, and rested
awhile and went on. But instead of turning to the right towards
Whittier's Ridge, I went straight on through the settlement, southward, intending to go to St Andrews and start for myself!" She
had covered quite a distance along this lonely road before realiz-
ing the magnitude of what she was doing: "I walked on a mile or
more past the last farm and was descending a hill where the road
entered a deep forest, when suddenly I came to myself with the
thought, *'Where am I going? What am I trying to do?'* I stopped
short, overwhelmed by a sense of the utter folly and madness of
my attempt. Blinded by a rush of tears, I turned to retrace my
steps, completely cured!" (Memoir, 26–7).

Fittingly, her epiphany comes at a satisfying "literary" moment: the point at which she is about to descend into the shadows of a deep wood. Having decided to abort her journey southward, she then had to return to the road she should have been travelling on, and the only way to do so was to cross the fields diagonally until she finally reached it. But to her chagrin, she was "seen and known,"

> and many were the surmises of the Clarence housewives, as to my field tramping. One woman called to me, but I did not hear. These surmises and enquiries came to Aunt Martha's, and from them to me, with many jokes and comments on my crazy walk. But I kept my folly to myself, merely intimating that "I forgot myself, and went the wrong road;" which was true in a sense, but not all the truth. Years afterward I told mother all about it; but others were never the wiser ... I was always much better content at home after that wild attempt to leave it. (Memoir, 27)

This passage is found in Sarah's memoir, which she wrote for her grown children in the final years of her life. Shortly before this anecdote, she tells of how she "met the Muse" and was overwhelmed by the desire to write poetry, and of how her poems were thought to be wonderful by some key family members. Given this context and the encouragement she received, it is likely that she left home to seek fame and fortune as a writer. From St Andrews she probably intended to sail to Boston or to New York, where both her father and her older brother often worked in the shipyards and had many friends and contacts.

For Sarah, the blossoming of her talents as a writer brought with it restlessness and a desire to escape the confines of her conservative rural community, to see the wider world and try on new identities. Educated at home, she wrote diaries and poems almost all her life and fashioned her memoir both from her memories and from surviving notes and diaries. Although she never became a famous writer, her voice shouts from every page, expressing by turns her rage, joy, obsessions, and grief. Her intellectual curiosity fired her imagination, and the scanty reading material available to her shaped her goals for years to come. It also influenced her literary style, giving her the basic structures of the novel (tension, climax, denouement) and the figurative language of poetry, all of which she clearly absorbed and deployed in her own writing. In her account here she also expresses a wish to escape the hard manual labour that farm women were doomed to perform. This included carding, spinning, and weaving wool from the family sheep for clothing, making butter and cheese, scrubbing floors, and washing heavy garments and bedding by hand every week, in all kinds of weather, without the assistance of even a wringer washing machine. What creative young woman would not wish to escape such drudgery?

Sarah's amusement at her adolescent dreams and her affection for her younger self are both evident in this passage from her memoir. What is particularly striking in her account is that the fourteen-year-old Sarah expects life to unfold like a novel – specifically an adventure story – despite the fact that the heroes of such stories were all boys. This tendency to see heroism and heroic models as available to her despite the gender boundaries that restricted nineteenth-century females was to characterize her ambitions for much of her life. Although the career paths of the literary characters she admired in these novels – lecturer, preacher, or doctor – would not have been open to her as a young woman in the 1850s, this reality clearly did not stop her from dreaming of a world where such options existed, and from eventually joining social movements that promised change. Indeed, one of her most powerful role models was a woman, Harriet N. Austin, who became both a doctor and a lecturer in these reform movements.

In fact, for much of her life Sarah channelled her longing for a better life into a utopian dream: creating a congenial community of reformers who adhered to the principles of water cure and dress reform. Proposed in an article in the alternative health magazine the *Herald of Health* in 1864 by Sarah's husband, Joel Bonney Craig, the scheme for a "Colony of Reformers" at one point involved an extensive correspondence with people all across North America. Revived briefly in the 1880s, the colony plan eventually collapsed under the weight of the Craigs' poverty and personal misfortune. But while Joel's enthusiasm for such a scheme waned, the dream never died for Sarah. Her quest for a better life haunted her for the rest of her life and led to her migrations westward after his death. The idea of a community of sympathetic minds gave way, as the years wore on, to the more modest goal of a stable environment in which to make a living and raise her large family. Determined to keep moving until she had found what she was looking for, Sarah ended her days on her own profitable fruit farm in the Okanagan in British Columbia, surrounded by the orchards of her children and neighbours, in an area of natural beauty and bounty reminiscent of that lost Eden that she had so long sought.

Although Sarah never realized her utopian dream, she chronicled its progress in her diaries and later, near the end of her life, in her lengthy memoir. Even in this reminiscence, composed fifty years after the demise of her colony scheme, her passion for the various causes she supported and her fiery determination to stand true to her beliefs leap off the page. Diaries written by poor rural women are rare in Canada; most farm wives had little time for or interest in recording their experiences, and the few who did so tended to document only the rudiments of their daily routines.[1] Sarah was different. Obsessed with reading and writing from an early age, she was a compulsive diarist for much of her life and was working on her carefully crafted memoir (which she called her "History") up until her death in 1919 at the age of seventy-nine.

In many ways, Sarah's highly personal account of her struggles with family and community gives voice to the normally unvoiced experience of other marginal women like her. Her descriptions of the desperate poverty of her daily existence afford us a glimpse of life at the bottom of the economic ladder, a perspective rarely articulated by other nineteenth-century diarists. At the same time, her obsession with ideas and her determination to be the architect of her own life mark her as a distinctive personality. Unlike many other nineteenth-century women diarists, Sarah boldly situates herself at the centre of her texts and constructs herself as a heroic figure battling the forces of ignorance. Her rhetoric emulates that of the educated, middle-class female reformers whose writings provided her with much-needed hope and inspiration for many years. Her passionate and at times highly rhetorical account of the colony scheme provides insights into an obscure grassroots movement that would otherwise be forgotten. And in her eloquent expression of her joys and sorrows as a wife and mother there is always a sense of her deliberate *crafting* of her experience.

Unlike many women diarists of her time, Sarah seems always to have intended these intimate accounts to be read, and she was consciously or even unconsciously shaping them for a future audience, even if the readers were only her children. And in shaping them for that audience, particularly in her memoir, Sarah – like many of her more highly educated counterparts – made use of the literary elements that were familiar to her.[2] Indeed, as scholars of women's life writing have recently observed, nineteenth-century women's diaries and memoirs were more likely than men's to emulate fictional models such as the novel, particularly the romantic novel with its happy ending.[3] They note that "by adopting elements from works of fiction a diarist can redefine the past, alter the perception of the present, and control the future."[4] These strategies are apparent throughout Sarah Craig's memoir in particular, but also in some sections of her diaries.

Her reformist impulses were a product of larger societal forces. Utopian communities were all the rage in nineteenth-century North America. As Emerson commented to Carlyle in 1840, "Not a reading man but has a draft of a new community in his waistcoat pocket."[5] Founded on principles that differed widely, only a handful of these colonies lasted more than a few months. Those that succeeded at all seemed to depend on charismatic leaders for their cohesiveness. But even the presence of such figures did not guarantee success; good economic management was also important if the group were to survive. Moreover, as Seymour Kesten points out, such communities were often plagued by illusions about colony life, by the lack of a clear working strategy, and by "foggy ideas about principles."[6] Many intentional communities fell apart because of incompatibility among members who naively believed that they would all automatically get along if they shared the same beliefs and goals. Indeed, the road to a new life in such colonies was strewn with pitfalls that utopian zealots inevitably failed to see. Their ironclad belief in the possibility of a "heaven on earth" often blinded them to the harsh realities of everyday life in a communal society.

The impulse to form intentional communities was part of a broader nineteenth-century belief that humankind was perfectible, that through education and effort each individual and eventually society itself could be transformed. Such an optimistic view was the basis for numerous reform movements in North America, including abolitionism, feminism, and temperance, all of which reflected a rising idealism. Although all these movements differed to some extent in their diagnosis of the key impediment to humanity's perfection and the right path toward it, the central impulse was the same.[7]

This idea of the perfectibility of humankind can be traced to the "humanist, rationalist course taken by religion" from the late eighteenth century onward, deeply influenced by the Enlightenment, in which God as the punisher of misdeeds was replaced by a more compassionate, fatherlike deity.[8] This shift had far-reaching implications, and the revivals and millennialist movements of the 1830s and 1840s can be seen as partly a reaction to this new view. The Enlightenment belief in science and progress bolstered the new confidence that perfection was within reach. Romanticism and the ideas of the French philosopher Jean-Jacques Rousseau combined to present an ideal of human perfection within a "natural" society.[9]

This new optimism also touched individuals in their everyday lives. For the first time, disease could be viewed not as God's punishment for misdeeds but as something avoidable, the cause of which could be discovered and eliminated. Escaping disease was thus not only possible but within God's loving plan. As James Whorton puts it, "Physical salvation, therefore, could be achieved as certainly as spiritual salvation if the individual exerted himself to understand God's edicts and then exercised the divine gifts of reason and free will to obey them. In fact, one had no moral alternative. The laws of health, the rules revealed by the science of physiology, were as binding as the Ten Commandments, so that healthful living was not just an opportunity, it was a religious duty."[10] What emerged was "a sort of Christian physiology," which interpreted science in light of Christian morality and was strongly influenced by the Romantic idealization of nature and the impulse toward restoring a pre-industrial "natural life."[11]

It is no accident, then, that so many of the nineteenth-century reform movements used the kind of evangelical language and tactics associated with popular religion. The linkages between evangelical Christianity and many of these groups, including those that advocated forming intentional communities, were very strong. The reform movements –temperance, phrenology, water cure, dress reform – emerged at the same time as waves of religious revival were sweeping North America. All these popular movements sought to establish some version of "the kingdom of Heaven on Earth."[12] One need only read the writings of Ellen G. White, founder of the Seventh-day Adventists, Mother Ann Lee of the Shakers, John Humphrey Noyes of the Oneida Community,

or Robert Owen of the New Harmony colony in Indiana to rec-
ognize the religious vocabulary common to all of them.[13] Even
the more secular utopian movements, such as the Transcenden-
talists, used some of the language of religion in articulating their
visions of the perfect society.

Not all believers in reform causes felt the need to organize
themselves into separate communities, but many did. Brook
Farm, New Harmony, and Fruitlands (co-founded by Louisa May
Alcott's father) were only three of the most famous failed utopian
experiments. Hundreds of others rose and fell without much
fanfare. By the mid-nineteenth century, only the Oneida Community could be seen as a success. Most of these colonies fell apart
when it became clear that they would never be economically
viable.[14] Given this dismal record, one might ask why a couple
of poverty-stricken, backwoods intellectuals like Sarah and her
husband would imagine that they could succeed in forming a
coherent community themselves. How could they expect to get
along well enough with a group of strangers to make such a
colony work? What factors made their life in southwestern New
Brunswick so unbearable that they would contemplate leaving
friends and family behind (likely forever) to begin a new life in an
unknown country with a diverse collection of people whom they
knew only through letters? And how was this tenacious idea able
to survive Joel's death and propel Sarah and her children into a
decades-long quest for a new, more congenial home, even if that
home was ultimately not the type of intentional community she
once envisioned?

This book seeks to illuminate such questions by focusing on
Sarah Jameson Craig's life writing, which (with the exception of a
twelve-year break) spans the years from her birth in 1840 and

childhood to shortly before her death in 1919. These narratives include descriptions of the failed colony scheme, as well as her accounts of her later migrations westward in search of a better life. Along the way she describes the frustrations of living in almost continuous poverty, within a society that offered few options for children educated at home (as hers were by necessity) and especially for females. She takes care to include poetic descriptions of the beauties of nature (a blueberrying expedition in New Brunswick, a winter mirage on the prairie, the soft green woodlands of the Okanagan), as well as lively accounts of the exploits of her children and grandchildren.

Sarah's is a rare articulate voice from the margins of rural Canada – a voice that is at once both ordinary and extraordinary. She is in many ways the typical rural farm wife struggling to raise a large brood of children. On the other hand, she is unusual among women of her class and time: poor, yet highly literate and well-read in the current medical theories of her day, and aware of currents of thought circulating far beyond the boundaries of home. Her life writing expresses her deep love for her husband and children, but also documents her persistent quest for a better life, from her adoption of the "reform dress" (a version of the Bloomer costume) at the age of seventeen, to her full-blown plans for a "Colony of Reformers" in the 1860s, to her restless search for a stable environment in which to raise her family as she moved westward later in life. Her resolute insistence on practising water-cure therapy for many years, despite heated confrontations with family members and neighbours alike, highlights her conviction that a better life was within reach. Sarah's accounts of some of her cures, published in the New York magazine the *Herald of Health*, together with her diary reports of other such cases, provide a

glimpse of her fiery determination and the opposition she perceived at home. Her concern with constructing herself as a heroic
figure in the face of implacable foes makes her writings all the
more interesting. Her implicit acceptance of more modest goals in
later life is nevertheless conveyed with ongoing passion and verve.

Sarah was an obsessive chronicler of her life and thoughts. Her
private writings, never before published, offer to the twenty-first-
century reader a glimpse into her inner life and the passion, ambition, and struggle that characterized her journey through
obscurity in nineteenth- and early twentieth-century Canada. The
trajectory of her physical journey from east to west is typical of a
common Canadian migration pattern in this period. However, it
is Sarah's *inner* journey – from the fiery idealist to the mellow
grandmother enjoying at last the fruitfulness of her Eden in that
longed-for west – that commands the most attention. Her desires,
forcefully articulated on paper, surely reflect in some measure the
desires of every woman in Canada during this time, and for this
reason she deserves to be heard.

Sarah Jameson Craig's writings survive in several forms: her
early diaries, beginning in 1865 (the first years reconstructed from
diaries lost in an 1865 fire) and continuing with some brief inter-
ruptions to 1889; her later diaries, from 1902 until her death in
1919; and her memoir, which she called her "History," written for
her family during the last two decades of her life and intended to
document her early years and those of her husband, Joel, and their
life together. The memoir is more carefully crafted and often more
literary than the diaries, but it covers only the years up to 1882; the
diaries continue for many more, ending just three weeks before
her death. Sarah reworked and augmented her diary material in
the memoir, which she intended as a legacy to her children; thus

she included in it much material about Joel's childhood as well as her own. The memoir survives both in Sarah's original handwriting and in the form of a typescript made in the 1960s by her youngest daughter, Florence, who fills in some of the details of events during the hiatus of twelve years between 1889 and 1902 (part 2 of the memoir); references throughout this book are to the pagination of this typescript. Sarah's abbreviations and her occasional spelling mistakes have been retained in all transcripts of the diaries. All these manuscripts, together with a diary kept for one year (1885) by Sarah's oldest daughter, Alice, and numerous photographs, are now housed in the Charlotte County Archives in St Andrews, New Brunswick.

Chapter One

Early Days and Influences

Sarah Jameson was born in 1840 in St Andrews, New Brunswick, the daughter of sailor, shipbuilder, and farmer Charles Jameson and his wife, Alice Woodin Jameson. (The family name was sometimes spelled Jamieson or Jamison.) She spent her first two years in a rented house in the seaside town of St Andrews, but her father soon moved the family about twenty miles north to a parcel of one hundred acres of Crown land that he had purchased in a heavily wooded area in the parish of St Patrick. It was this sparsely settled landscape, with its hardwood forests and scattered farms, that would be Sarah's home for the next forty-five years of her life. Like many rural New Brunswickers, Charles Jameson derived his income only partly from the farm; for most of the year, he worked away from home as a shipbuilder, often across the border in Maine. He also fished, built his own boats, and sold them if he got a good offer (Memoir, 17). Other inhabitants of the area survived by working in the lumber camps for part of the year. Despite the uneven quality of the land, many settlers in the villages of Whittier's Ridge, Pleasant Ridge, Clarence Hill, and Rolling Dam made a passable living by combining farming with other activities.[1]

While they were linked to St Andrews in a number of ways, these rural villages seem to have had even stronger ties with St Stephen to the west and with Calais, the American town across the St Croix River. It was to St Stephen that many of the farmers took their butter and produce to sell, and it was across the river in Calais that they bought fabric for clothing or had their pictures taken at the ambrotype studio. Then, as now, the towns along the St Croix River and around Passamaquoddy Bay formed one "social and geographic unity."[2] Indeed, since many of the settlers in this part of New Brunswick (including Sarah Jameson's family) were descendants of United Empire Loyalists, this affinity is not surprising. The international boundary was merely an arbitrary line, and the influence of American goods and ideas was a natural part of the ebb and flow of trade across the border.

In a contribution to *The Jamesons in America*, published in 1901, which traces the lineage and fortunes of the various branches of the Jameson clan, Sarah describes her childhood home in a piece she calls "Memory Glimpses":

How well I remember that sunny little spot in the wilds! The "clearing" of a few acres, carpeted with green, in which stood the little log cabin, with its crevices filled with moss, its roof of spruce bark instead of shingles, its one door and two single-sash windows. Within was a single room, a stone fireplace, with its hearth of broad, flat stones, which half filled one end, where in cold weather glowed the old-fashioned fire … In one back corner stood mother's bed, with the children's trundle-bed rolled under it in the daytime, and a table, cupboard, a few chairs, and two chests, all home-made and painted, our father's handiwork … Such was my childhood's home in the backwoods of Charlotte County, N.B., to which my parents removed when I was eighteen months old, and a happy home it was![3]

Sarah's father and the other settlers cleared the land, burning the trees there on the ground, and planted crops around the blackened stumps and logs. On this farm Charles Jameson raised ten children, of whom Sarah was the oldest surviving daughter.

This early home was situated in an area of great natural beauty, with many ridges and mountains offering breathtaking views, some of which Sarah describes in loving detail in her memoir: "Away to the North glisten the blue Oromocto Lakes … Glimpses of rivers and streams flash out among miles and leagues of unbroken forest; while away to the North-west we can see Mt Katahdin and the white saddleback of Mt Palfrey in Maine" (18). This land also offered its own natural bounty in summer and fall, with plenty of wild strawberry, cranberry, and blueberry bushes, along with wild cherry and pear trees, all producing buckets of fruit to be picked by whoever was willing, and wild hay waiting for the men to cut and cure. Every family who owned woodland had sugar maple trees and routinely harvested the syrup in spring.

Nevertheless, the community's remote situation brought challenges as well: St Stephen was nearly a twenty-mile walk or ride from Whittier's Ridge, Rolling Dam, Pleasant Ridge, and Clarence Hill, and St Andrews was just as far to the south. The inhabitants of these tiny villages lacked many of the amenities that other nineteenth-century rural areas enjoyed: there was no post office at first and, until later in the century, no school. Roads were rough, and winter storms often made them impassable; plowing out the snow was left to the inhabitants themselves. Until later in the century there was also no rail line. Education was generally left to the parents and, in consequence, was a hit-and-miss affair. Many of the inhabitants were barely literate. Very few owned a book.

Sarah Jameson was lucky: her father believed firmly in the education of his children through whatever means was available. Although his wife, Sarah's mother, could not write well, she was a good reader, and between them the two parents made sure their children became literate. From the beginning Sarah was very eager to learn to write, and she claims that she "would confiscate every bit or scrap of blank paper I got hold of ... to write on" with the goose quills that her father made (Memoir, 21). The Bible served as the primary text, but there was other reading material in the home as well. In another contribution published in *The Jamesons in America*, she describes her early education: "The settlers were too few to afford a school, so our parents taught us at home reading, writing, and arithmetic, and encouraged to study and master other branches as we were able. Our little shelf of books was my special delight. Passionately fond of study and writing, I made the most of every moment available for such employment, so it happened that I never attended, or saw the inside of, a day school until I was called to teach a little school myself."[4]

The school that she refers to here was held in her parents' home. It had been established at the encouragement of John G. Lorimer, former editor of the *Provincial Patriot* newspaper, who published two of Sarah's poems when she was only sixteen. Having just been appointed county school inspector, he paid a call to the Jameson house and, "deciding that I was capable of teaching the few children of the place, told me I should gather them together, and start a little school in our front room. This I was very willing to do, hoping it would prove a stepping stone to a larger teachership; thus opening the doors to a wider education for myself, while I started others on the same road" (Memoir, 35).

Sarah managed to recruit a few children, although a number of families were "amused and indifferent" at the thought of a girl who had never attended a school herself presuming to teach others. Nevertheless, the little school prospered for a while:

> I heartily enjoyed my work, and could note a marked improvement in my pupils day by day. Mother advised that until I had proved my ability to teach and so won the confidence of the people of the place, I should offer to teach for only the cost of my board: but even that was withheld or given grudgingly, though we took it in farm produce. The Inspector wrote me that he could not get me a License, or an allowance from the Government for teaching in my father's house; and he advised that the people build a little house for my school. But we knew that no such house would be built at that time. (Memoir, 35)

The other settlers might allow their children to attend a school, but they did not value education enough to build or pay for one. As a result, Sarah taught for only three months and then returned to her routine household life helping her mother, whose work was "never done." This would be only the first of many opportunities missed because of lack of funds.

Nevertheless, Sarah became not only literate but relatively well-educated through home study, as did most of her siblings. All of them learned to read and write. Her youngest brother, Edwin, who at not quite four years old was the smartest pupil in her home school, would move to Buffalo, New York, when he grew up and become a successful printer, writing witty letters home to his sister's children.

Sarah herself had a larger ambition: to be a great writer. Her obsession with crafting language marked her from an early age. Her earliest poem, apparently composed shortly before she ran away from home, was about spring. She notes in her memoir, "When I put this effusion on paper, it was thought wonderful by several of the family and others; and I now believed myself a genius – an embryo Poet, destined to develop into a full-fledged child of the Muse; climb the rocky steep of Fame, and write my name among the earth's great ones! Every subject or object that appealed very strongly to my mind or feelings was thenceforward wrought into verse or rhyme" (26). In *The Jamesons in America* she characterizes her early writing ambitions in these words: "I used to write rhymes and poems when a girl and occasionally later; and was thought by myself and friends to be a poet indeed; my highest ambition for years being to see my name set high among the poetical stars of the century. But the dream faded, as life with its stern realities took its place; though I never wholly gave up the muse."[5]

This calm account obscures the passion for writing that emerges even from Sarah's memoir, written so many years later, and especially in her account of her attempt to run away, quoted earlier. Her dreams of being a writer never really died, but it was only in the last decades of her life that she was finally paid anything for her writing. Who knows what path her life might have taken if a broad education had been available to her? In a different time and place she could at least have trained as a teacher. As it was, the reading material that chanced across her path proved a potent, formative force in Sarah's life. Although the novels she refers to in the passage describing her aborted "escape" from home were clearly influential, it was the magazines and other periodicals that she was exposed to which literally changed her life.

Like their father, her older brother Albert was a shipbuilder and worked for a time across the border in Maine. While there, he subscribed to a couple of Boston weeklies and brought these and other newspapers and magazines home on his visits. The young Sarah devoured this material, especially the magazines devoted to what she termed "new fields of science and useful knowledge": "Most important of those were the 'Phrenological Journal,' teaching mental science and mind reading by the shape of the head, etc; and the 'Water Cure Journal,' teaching hygiene – the science and laws of health – as far as then known; and a new Healing Art, which entirely repudiated drugs as *curatives*, and was then called 'Water Cure,' though water was only *one* of the agents employed in healing by the exponents of the system" (Memoir, 30). This early exposure to two of the most influential reform movements of the nineteenth century had a profound effect on Sarah Jameson. It was to mould her character and beliefs for decades to come. It was also to inform her writing style: unlike many nineteenth-century female writers, she was not reticent about stating her opinions or speaking about herself. Like the other contributors to the *Water-Cure Journal*, she wrote openly about her thoughts and feelings and even the intimate events of her life, such as her multiple childbirths.

Although the connections between phrenology and water cure (or hydropathy) may seem tenuous to the modern reader, in fact the two movements were linked by many common interests. Phrenology not only claimed that a person's physical and mental character was revealed in the shape of his or her skull, but also that by exercising certain mental functions, character could be improved and faults overcome.[6] O.S. and L.N. Fowler, the prophets of phrenology in the United States, claimed that their new science opened the way for the improvement of the entire human race, an ideal that firmly aligned their beliefs with the other "perfectionist" movements of the day. Linking phrenology with physiology, they urged reform in many areas of health, including women's dress, exercise and diet, and temperance.[7] Both phrenology and hydropathy also affirmed the concept that women were intellectually equal to men, and thus aligned themselves with the nascent women's rights movement.[8] O.S. Fowler, who became one of the editors of the *American Phrenological Journal*, was a wholehearted supporter of water cure.[9] He often reprinted articles from the *Water-Cure Journal* (later renamed the *Herald of Health*) and carried advertisements for that periodical. The editors of the *Water-Cure Journal* reciprocated by advertising the *American Phrenological Journal* on their back pages. Fowler frequently contributed articles to the *Water-Cure Journal*, and when it ran into financial trouble, he rescued the publication from oblivion.[10] As the back-cover advertisement for the *Water-Cure Journal and Herald of Reforms* in the *American Phrenological Journal* of January 1849 specified, the publication of the two magazines was made to coincide. Clearly, each shared a large segment of the other's readership, and since the *Water-Cure Journal* was "one of the most widely read health periodicals of its day,"[11] this degree of overlap ensured a broad audience for both.

Hydropathy enjoyed a huge popularity in the first half of the nineteenth century. As a system of alternative medicine, it advocated the use of water, applied both externally and internally, to treat diseases of all kinds. The movement flourished in reaction to the shortcomings of conventional nineteenth-century medical practitioners, or "allopaths," as water-cure enthusiasts called them, most of whom relied on interventionist methods (such as bleeding and blistering) and alcohol-based drugs.[12] By the early nineteenth century people in all sectors of society had come to regard many of these medical interventions as more harmful than helpful; certainly they were almost never pleasant.[13] Hydropathy, with its emphasis on pure soft water as nature's primary therapeutic agent, offered a more comfortable path to healing. Most importantly, it sought to aid the body's own natural healing processes.

First popularized by the Austrian peasant Vincent Priessnitz in early nineteenth-century Graefenberg, the water-cure movement spread to North America in the 1840s. Two of the founders of the movement in the United States, Joel Shew and Russell Thatcher Trall, in 1843–44 opened a water-cure house in New York, where they put Priessnitz's methods into use. The other important advocate in the United States, Mary Gove Nichols, established the American Hydropathic College in 1849 to train men and women physicians in water-cure methods. These three became the central figures in the early development of hydropathy in North America.[14]

Priessnitz believed that "health was a natural condition and disease an unnatural one."[15] If left alone, the body was able to heal itself; but this process could be aided by the judicious application of water. It was through the skin, Priessnitz believed, that diseases passed out of the body. Thus "applications of water, wraps, sweating, and applying pressure and friction cleansed and opened the pores, aided circulation, invigorated the skin, and drew the putrid matter out of the body."[16] The centrepiece of the system was the wet-sheet pack, which "sought to restore balance to the system by inducing a 'crisis,' … Hydropathic leaders, including Trall and Shew, saw the process as a drawing out of bad elements and their replacement with healthy elements."[17] The wet-sheet pack was used at some stage in the treatment of almost every illness because it supposedly served as a "conduit" for these elements of disease to pass out of the body. It also produced pleasant effects: "While the wet-sheet pack had an initial shock of cold, it quickly produced a feeling of physical well-being and often a sedated deep sleep. This procedure was performed by having the patient lie on the sheet, which had been dipped in cold water, wrung out, and placed on top of four blankets. The patient was wrapped first in the wet sheet and then in each blanket in turn. Every body part was covered except the face; the result was a mummylike encasement."[18] If more heat was needed – for instance, if the patient was very cold – additional blankets or even hot water bottles could be added until the patient began to perspire. After a period of time inside the pack, the patient was advised to immediately bathe in cold or tepid water and then to be rubbed down to stimulate the circulation.[19] The fact that this process usually left the patient feeling rested and refreshed was likely one of its strongest recommendations.

Although the basic assumption that the human body needed to maintain balance in order to remain disease-free characterized *both* allopathic and hydropathic medicine, the hydropaths' insistence on disease as preventable, and on the individual's ability to act to achieve that prevention, accounted for much of the water-cure system's attraction. But hydropaths also seized on the general discontent with the discomforts and dangers of allopathic methods. At a time when orthodox medicine was barely regulated, they developed a full-blown rhetoric of warfare against the "drug-doctors," whom they portrayed not as simply ineffectual but as misguided and evil. Their message was bolstered by the presence in the movement's leadership of former allopaths such as William Andrus Alcott and Russell Thatcher Trall, who were "converted" to the water-cure system after wandering in "the wilderness of pills and powders" for years.[20]

As the water-cure movement became established in North America, some of Priessnitz's methods were modified by practitioners who found that patients often reacted badly to the stronger treatments such as cold-water baths. Soon tepid water was being used instead, and more attention was paid to the individual patient's reactions and needs.[21] Articles advocating the warm bath as an alternative treatment appeared in the *Water-Cure Journal*. Although the arguments presented focused on results, there was also an underlying concern to make the therapy more agreeable and therefore more attractive to a wide range of patients.[22]

From the standpoint of the twenty-first century, the claim that water could be used in treating all diseases seems preposterous. Yet it must be remembered that it was not until the late nineteenth century that the germ theory of disease was at all accepted in medical circles; even the discoveries of Pasteur and Koch in the 1860s and 1870s did not turn the tide immediately, and the significance of micro-organisms was hotly debated for decades. Until germs were identified, nobody knew for certain what caused diseases to attack the human body. Indeed, for many centuries, little real progress had been made in the understanding of sickness and how it spreads.[23] The hydropaths of the 1850s and 1860s were working from a model of human physiology that was as flawed as that of their more orthodox rivals, but they certainly understood no *less* about the causes of illness than the allopaths did. Their emphasis on bathing and proper diet caused no harm and likely improved the general health of many of their patients in an age when hygiene was not a priority. Indeed, ignorance of basic hygienic practices was apparently so widespread that an 1858 article in the *Water-Cure Journal* discussed "Reasons for Bathing" in great detail.

Perhaps most important to water-cure patients were the psychological benefits: they were encouraged to take control of their own bodies and engage in a program of healthy living that would prevent disease from arising in the first place. This approach was a radical shift from the methods of the conventional doctors, who intervened with drugs and bleeding only when disease was already present, and in whose supposedly "expert" hands the patient was passive and dependent. By empowering patients with knowledge and practical methods for taking care of themselves, the water-cure system placed the potential for healthy living within the hands of the average person, rather than with expensive medical "experts."

Susan Cayleff has suggested that the American "emphasis on self-care" accounts in large part for the receptive audience that Priessnitz's ideas received in the United States in the early nineteenth century.[24] This may be true, but the fact that water was cheap and readily available, and that people of low and average incomes everywhere could more easily afford the treatment than drug medications, was undoubtedly also a prime reason for its popularity. While patients with the means to do so could go to water-cure establishments to be treated, hydropathy was actively marketed as a system that could be easily learned for home use. Eager to promote hydropathy to the masses, the *Water-Cure Journal* included in its first few issues a series of articles that described the basics of the method.[25] In 1849 the journal published "The Water-Cure Processes Illustrated," which presented the principal steps of the hydropathic system accompanied by illustrations.[26] The journal also carried advertisements for syringes (to be used to give enemas as needed) and the sheets required for the wet-sheet pack, which could be purchased at reasonable prices. There was always a column called "Water-Cure at Home," and the journal regularly offered advice to those who wrote in with descriptions of their illnesses. Hydropathy thus demystified medical care by taking it out of the hands of the doctors and placing it in the hands of the self-educated person at home. This idea of taking responsibility for one's own health still resonates in our own time in numerous alternative health practices.

Although Joel Shew promoted a rigorous version of the vegetarian diet devised by Sylvester Graham (father of the Graham cracker) as part of his water-cure regimen – and, indeed, seems to have borrowed much of his diet advice from Graham's book *Lectures on the Science of Human Life* – it was Russell Thatcher Trall who enlarged the scope of the water cure's concerns beyond treating disease to preventing it in the first place.[27] It was Trall who developed hydropathy into "a comprehensive healing philosophy" by linking it with diet, exercise, and physiology in general.[28] As the American version of hydropathy evolved, it came to encompass a complete change of lifestyle to one requiring only simple foods, fresh air, and exercise for both men and women. But beyond this emphasis, hydropathy also consciously linked itself with a variety of other reformist ideas, including temperance, and, through its particular focus on women's health, with early feminist movements. Historian Sidney Ditzion comments that eventually "vegetarians, phrenologists, water-cure doctors, and anti-tobacco, anti-corset, and temperance people were to cross paths so frequently that they began to look like participants in a single reform movement."[29]

Trall's insistence on the benefits of hydropathy in childbirth and the care of babies undoubtedly consolidated the movement's support among women. In fact, from the beginning, the leaders of the movement recognized the water cure's potential attraction to women and its dependence on female support for any continued success. Accordingly, many articles in the *Water-Cure Journal* were targeted directly at women and their duties as mothers. Hydropathy particularly emphasized a woman's ability to understand and take care of her own body. Hydropaths repudiated the idea, common among regular physicians, that a woman was "weaker" than a man and that she required the knowledge of "expert" physicians.[30] Especially repugnant was the orthodox definition of pregnancy as a "disease" that routinely required medical intervention. Instead, hydropaths argued that pregnancy and childbirth were perfectly natural functions for which the female body was uniquely designed.[31] Instead of relying on often ill-informed male doctors, the pregnant health reformer was encouraged to involve herself in a complete program of prenatal, natal, and postnatal care, perhaps assisted by a female hydropath but always remaining in control of the whole process of childbirth.[32] Understandably, women found this philosophy empowering. Indeed, after the birth of her fifth child with only a half-hour of real labour, Sarah Craig asserted in her diary, "When women ... understand and obey all God's physical and mental laws, children will be born without the least degree of suffering or danger" (Early diaries, 26 June 1867). Here she echoes a claim frequently made by hydropaths in their literature.

Hydropathy also actively encouraged women to take on the role of healer and thus expand their private caregiving functions within the family to the public arena. In accordance with the increasingly popular idea of woman's "moral superiority," health reformers preached that her influence was needed to reshape and purify society as a whole.[33] Besides, they argued, women were by nature particularly suited to the healing arts. Mary Gove Nichols, the movement's most powerful female role model and herself a hydropathic physician, declared in one article that women were particularly well fitted to the practice of medicine because of their natural kindness, patience, and "tenderer love."[34] Although this idea may seem to simply reinforce the stereotype of the idealized domestic female, the message was in fact a powerful one at a time when women were shut out of most regular medical schools. The few who did persevere in seeking medical training were often subjected to ridicule and abuse and denied opportunities to practise. Elizabeth Blackwell is only one famous example of a female medical graduate who was refused placement in a hospital at the end of her training. The assertion that women were *by nature* better fitted to be medical doctors openly challenged the chauvinism of the male medical schools.[35]

All these aspects of the health-reform movement combined to attract the young Sarah Jameson. In a remote rural community where self-reliance was an absolute necessity in daily life and where women often ran the farm while husbands and sons worked away, the ideal of a natural, healthy life attainable through one's own efforts and available to all was a powerful one. Like many other converts to the water-cure system, Sarah relied on reading the movement's magazines and tracts for her information. Unfortunately, her keen interest in these subjects was often thwarted by her family's poverty.

> I could find no way of obtaining money to subscribe for one or both journals, as I wished to do; though the price of each was one dollar per year. Father was a lover of good reading, but had never felt able to pay for a paper; feeling that when he could hardly provide the family with plain food and clothing, we must take what chance we could for reading. When he was away at work, and sending his savings home, mother still had to spend the dollars *very* carefully; to have one donation reach till the next came. So though she became very much interested in the new studies, she could give no financial help. She joined me in studying when she could; and we put in practice as we could our newly gained knowledge of hygiene, in regard to diet, bathing, etc. (Memoir, 30)

Sarah's cousin Joel Bonney Craig, who lived nearby and who would later become her husband, was also an enthusiastic student of these new sciences and a frequent visitor and partner in study. But his family was even poorer than Sarah's, since his mother was a widow.

> His means were very scanty; but he pinched out a few shillings a few times, to pay for a book or paper to help our studies and give us interesting light. Once, walking home from Chamcook, just at a spot where he and Isaac had found a piece of money, a year ago that day, he thought, "I wonder

if I'll find money here today"; and glancing down saw at his feet several pieces of silver in the mud. When cleaned, it counted nine shillings and sixpence, ($1.90). This he applied to increase our stock of Hygiene reading. I say "our," for whatever he or we obtained of good reading was held as common property; he being as a brother in our family. (Memoir, 31)

Sarah's and Joel's intense interest in the healing properties of water had much to do with a knee injury that Joel had received in his youth, which healed badly as a result of improper cleansing. While he was felling trees, his axe slipped and gashed his knee, and to prevent the cut from "taking cold," one of the men working with him "thrust into it a quid of tobacco from his mouth, tying it up with a dirty handkerchief" (Memoir, 2). The wound became infected and healed only very slowly, leaving Joel crippled for life. Rage at this disability, which could have been so easily prevented with the proper use of hygiene, was undoubtedly the most personal reason behind Sarah's and Joel's passionate adherence to methods of water cure. Certainly, the effects of this one injury continued to marginalize them economically for the rest of Joel's life.

Hydropathy was not the only radical measure to attract the young Sarah Jameson. Her new studies also included the writings of dress reformers, who, like the phrenologists, were aligned with the water-cure movement.

I soon learned that the way women dressed was unhealthful, uncomfortable, as well as inconvenient; their fettering, hampering, *monstrous* skirts gathering and holding damp and filth, and their tightly compressed waists, excluding the air

from the lungs, being positively and constantly disease producing ... The hooped skirt was but a reaction from the
heavy quilted petticoat, and while kept within reasonable
limits was an improvement. But my fellow students and I,
having come in touch with the Dress Reform movement,
had learned of a better, truer style of dress – more nearly
patterned after the form it was to cover; some of the ablest
hygienists being practical dress reformers, glorifying God
in their bodies as in their spirits. The more we studied, the
more deeply were we convinced that the "Bloomer dress"
and its improved successor, the "American Costume," were
incomparably better than the common mode, in freedom
of lungs, limbs and movements, in cost – in fact, in *every*
respect except popularity. And seeing an army of heroic
women, willingly, gladly, stemming the tide of popular
opinion by voice and pen and attire, to help emancipate
our sex from the thraldom of fashion, I resolved as soon
as possible to join them. (Memoir, 35–6)

Sarah's rhetoric in this passage mimics that of the reformers she
was reading. Her militaristic image of the "army of heroic women"
is borrowed from them, and it reveals the combative attitude that
would continue to characterize her writing on the subject for
many years. It also suggests much about the image of herself and
of her cause that she wished to present to her children years later,
when she was writing her memoir for them.

Sarah was, in fact, the first young woman in her community
to wear a "reform dress" when she adopted it at the age of seventeen. Her younger sister, Martha, also wore a version of the costume, but because she was still a child, the outfit looked enough

1.1 Sarah Jameson Craig in her reform dress about 1862

1.2 Martha Jameson in her reform dress about 1860

like the "frock and pantalettes" for children that it provoked little comment. For Sarah, as a young woman, the act of wearing the reform costume was a more radical move. She knew beforehand that this mode of dress would mark her unmistakeably in the eyes of the community: "I had counted the cost, and knew it would make me unpopular, an object of ridicule among our neighbors; and despised and scorned by others. But knowing the cause to be worthy, I did not hesitate to put myself and my influence with the noble minority facing public sentiment for the sake of right" (Memoir, 36). She faced no opposition at home; her mother approved, and her father, who was away working most of the time anyway, did not seem to mind and, indeed, favoured almost any style but hoops (Memoir, 36). But other members of the community often taunted her, and she was subjected to "some annoyance on the road … from certain 'rude fellows of the baser sort'" when she walked from village to village (Memoir, 42). Her grandmother believed the outfit to be "utterly sinful – an abomination to the Lord; who commanded through Moses that a woman should not wear garments 'pertaining to a man'" (Memoir, 36). Consequently, Sarah wore a long dress when visiting her grandmother and her aunt Martha (Joel Craig's mother), who was also scandalized by her new style of dress. Yet even years later, when writing her memoir, she stalwartly defended her choice: "But knowing fully, as I still know, that the principle of the reform was sound – grounded in truth, and a part of it – I adhered to its practice, backed by a few friends at and near home; and by words of cheer from the leaders, and the rank and file of the movement abroad" (Memoir, 36). The fact that these leaders were far away in New York and Boston and nowhere near at hand apparently made little difference to this

fervent young woman, who clearly saw herself as part of a significant social movement that extended well beyond the boundaries
of her rural community.

Dress reform was certainly a popular topic in the pages of the
Water-Cure Journal in the 1850s. The year 1851 saw the publication of both Mary Gove Nichols's "Lecture on Woman's Dresses"
in the August issue and the first of a series of articles, published
over several years, on women's clothing by Rachel Brooks Gleason,
who was one of the very few women with a medical degree in the
United States at that time.[36] Gleason pointedly asks, "Would men
wear clothing so uncomfortable and inconvenient as ours and
not complain?"[37] The answer was obvious. In October of the same
year the journal published an illustration captioned "The American and French Fashions Contrasted," depicting an uncorseted
woman in a short dress and trousers next to one wearing an elab-
orate wasp-waisted, low-necked gown of the period, along with
a diagram showing how dangerously constricted the rib cage and
waist of a corseted woman would be. Even conventional doctors
had for years been warning of the harm caused to the liver, lungs,
and reproductive system by wearing tightly laced corsets, which
often resulted in a twenty-inch waist, but their warnings seem to
have had little effect on fashionable women.[38] Even pregnant
women wore corsets; in fact, there were special maternity corsets
designed to be less rigid but yet allow the woman to hide her
pregnancy as long as possible, as Victorian values demanded.[39]
With the rise of the health-reform movement, prominent female
hydropathic physicians such as Mary Gove Nichols, Ellen Beard
Harman, Lydia Sayer Hasbrouck, and Harriet Austin urged pregnant women to abandon their corsets and, if possible, stay at

water-cure retreats such as Glen Haven and Elmira, where they could wear the comfortable reform costume without being exposed to critical eyes and thus pressured to put on the more constricting conventional dress.[40]

The articles in the *Water-Cure Journal* and other reformist magazines elicited an enthusiastic response, with women writing in to ask for specific directions on how to make a reform dress. James Caleb Jackson, an ardent water-cure supporter and eventual founder of the facility in Dansville, New York, known as Our Home on the Hillside, sponsored a dress-reform convention at his Glen Haven Water Cure in 1855, at which the National Dress Reform Association was founded. Although not required, the reform dress was worn by many patients at water-cure institutions, and in fact the female physicians who worked at these facilities considered it their duty as role models to wear the costume themselves and to lecture their patients on its physical advantages. As a result, any patient (male or female) who stayed at a water-cure establishment was immediately confronted with women wearing the short dress.[41]

The road to transforming women's fashion was not an easy one, however. Wearers faced hostility and ridicule from all quarters. Objections to the outfit worn by Elizabeth Cady Stanton, Amelia Bloomer, and reformers like them in the late 1840s and 1850s centred around the costume's masculine look. Many advocates modified the costume to make it more attractive, doing away with the wide Turkish pants and substituting straight-cut trousers instead.[42] Women were encouraged to retain feminine touches such as lace collars and jewellery, so as to avoid the charge of "masculinity."[43] Photographs of famous dress reformers such as Harriet Austin and Lydia Sayer Hasbrouck in their American Costumes show them wearing such feminine accessories.

No. 1. THE AMERICAN COSTUME.   No. 2   THE FRENCH COSTUME.

The American and French Fashions Contrasted.

We herewith present our readers with engraved views of the prevailing European and [proposed] American Fashions.

No. 1 represents Mrs. AMELIA BLOOMER, of Seneca Falls, N. Y. It was engraved from a Daguerreotype for the *Cayuga Chief*, an excellent newspaper published in Auburn, N. Y., and kindly loaned to us by Mr. THURLOW W. BROWN, the gentlemanly proprietor.

No. 2 was copied by our own Engraver, from the *Illustrated London News*, and is an *exact* copy of the original, without variation; and is a perfect representation of the FRENCH FASHIONS, as worn in July last. We submit the two styles side by side, for the consideration of AMERICAN WOMEN.

No. 3.—A NATURAL WAIST.

We also append, as an accompaniment, the anatomical views of a *natural* waist and an *artificial* or tight-laced waist, corresponding with Numbers 1 and 2 of the larger figures.

To us these views convey an unanswerable argument, and will need no further comment.

In future numbers we shall present other styles of the AMERICAN COSTUME, with patterns and appropriate descriptions accompanying them.

We should add in this connection, that the friends of Mrs. Bloomer do not regard the above as a *good* likeness of that lady; but as it conveys a *general* idea of the new costume, we consider it well adapted to our present purpose.

NO. 4.—A TIGHT-LACED WAIST.

1.3 "The American and French Fashions Contrasted,"
from the *Water-Cure Journal* of October 1851

1.4 Harriet Austin in the American Costume

Yet even these womanly touches did little to endear the outfit to the masses of North American women in an era when clear distinctions between masculine and feminine identities were seen as imperative. Since at this time career options for women were few and femininity was "a commodity on the marriage market," most women could not risk jeopardizing their feminine image in this way.[44] Further, as Jennifer Curtis notes, "by discarding the skirt, symbolic of womanhood, to assume pants, symbolic of male

1.5 Harriet Austin in another version of the reform dress

power, the Bloomer costume required a certain sacrifice of the female sense of self, and on a deeper level suggested femininity and empowerment could not coexist."[45]

Although Sarah gives no indication that she felt she was sacrificing her female identity, she describes the level of public hostility that her costume provoked. She records an incident in which she was threatened with arrest (albeit as a joke) while shopping with her mother in Calais, Maine, in 1865:

> The town was swarming, almost, with the "Boys in Blue" – returned soldiers in long, light blue overcoats; which were more conspicuous than my short skirt and pants. One of the blue-coats accosted us on the side-walk, and speaking very seriously, – addressing mother, as he thought I was but a girl – warned us that I was running a great risk appearing in that dress in public, when the police all through the country were searching for John Wilkes Booth, the murderer of Lincoln; intimating that *I might be arrested*! But his mask was too thin; we could see plainly he was only after a lark for himself and mates. I was told later that in Leaman's Ambrotype rooms, on Main Street, a man watched the window with a camera at the ready, trying for hours to get a view of me as we passed and repassed; but I was always moving too fast, and he failed! What a pity! (Memoir, 63)

It is important to note that when Sarah made and wore her reform dress, she had never actually seen one in real life. Unlike the many middle- and upper-class women who were introduced to the costume at one of the water-cure establishments where they had gone for treatment, Sarah had never met another dress reformer. All her information came from the articles and draw-ings in the pages of the *Water-Cure Journal* and any of the other reformist papers that crossed her path. These might have included some issues of the *Sibyl*, edited by Lydia Sayer Hasbrouck, a peri-odical dedicated to the dress-reform cause whose masthead featured a drawing of a woman in the short dress and trousers. Still, it is perhaps remarkable that Sarah's own version of the American Costume (see figure 1.1) so closely resembles outfits worn by famous dress reformers such as Harriet Austin.

In the autumn of 1858 Sarah and her brother George and cousin Joel walked twenty-five miles to Calais, Maine, to hear lectures by the renowned phrenologists L.N. Fowler and Dr S.R. Wells, whose books and magazines they had been studying. They arrived and introduced themselves to Fowler, "but when the Pro-fessor learned that we had really walked twenty-five miles to hear *one* lecture – the free one – his surprise was amusing. We had not thought it anything wonderful to do, with such an inducement; but he did" (Memoir, 39). Fowler was so impressed by the zeal of these young people that he handed them complimentary tickets to all his lectures on phrenology, and he "read" Sarah's head for free. This event was clearly one of the highlights of her young life; it was her first foray into the public arena of the "new science," her first chance to actually discuss these ideas with one of the experts of the day. Joel was able to attend only a few of the lectures before returning to work, but Sarah stayed on at Fowler's entreaty. "George and I spent the week, I at least drinking in new facts, thoughts, and ideas from the fountain of knowledge, faster than I could analyze or hold them. It was a long, delightful feast – a "feast of reason and flow of soul"; but as at a long-drawn-out banquet one is apt to eat more than one can digest or assimilate, so I imbibed more knowledge than I could retain; though I did not get mental indigestion" (Memoir, 40).

According to Sarah, Fowler proposed taking her with him back to New York to train in phrenology, but she knew that her mother could not spare her from home. Nevertheless, she went back to her community feeling richer than before: "We had acquired a new supply of material for study, sufficient for the winter, if we mastered it all. We did study eagerly, especially Joel and myself; and would almost have turned the community into a big school of Phrenology, if we could. But the people did not take to abstruse study, though they liked their 'bumps felt'" (Memoir, 41).

During the following months, Sarah and Joel continued to study whatever material they could get their hands on. Money was always a problem:

> Joel was a subscriber to the "Laws of Life," a fearless exponent of Hygienic Medication and Dress Reform, published at "Our Home," Dansville, N.Y. That summer [1859], someone sent me samples of "The Reformer," a new monthly, more decidedly radical still, on these great questions. I coaxed mother to *lend me the hens*, made them lay faster, and got money – one dollar – to subscribe. Writing occasionally for these papers, we came to be known to the editors and readers of that class of literature as strong and fearless thinkers along certain new lines. (Memoir, 42)

By the summer of 1858 Sarah and Joel's shared interests had ripened into romance and an agreement to marry when they could. This decision, too, led to discord. Joel was a poor man with a crippled leg, a serious disability in a rural area where heavy physical work was a basic requirement for men, whether in lumbering or in farming. As his widowed mother's only surviving child, he was barely able to make a living at various odd jobs. His ability to support a wife and family was seriously in doubt. Sarah writes: "Mother, who had guessed my secret, was very glad to know that my heart was satisfied. But when father came home in late Autumn, he treated the matter as altogether preposterous – a piece of child's folly. Joel's character and morals, and manner of life were above reproach; he was respected by all who knew him: but he was so very poor that father and some others thought for him to marry a dowerless wife would be next to madness!" (Memoir, 38).

Despite her father's misgivings, Sarah was adamant and continued her preparations for marriage, but it was not until 1860 that the wedding took place. Typically, poverty intervened. Sarah and Joel were married across the border in Calais, Maine, rather than in St Stephen, because in Calais they did not need a licence, which cost several dollars in New Brunswick (Memoir, 43). They had planned to be wed on New Year's Day in 1860, but could not do so because the snow was not deep enough for sleighing. At last on 26 January they set off, with a load of shingles in the sleigh for Joel to sell in Calais. They travelled all night, crossed the toll bridge before dawn so as not to have to pay, and were married at 3:00 p.m. in the home of a friend. But the reservations of family members cast a cloud over their union: "Albert had sent home $50.00, and of this father gave me $4.00 and a pair of shoes; for though he did not approve of our marriage, he would not let me go quite empty handed. Joel's mother must have known of our intentions; but I tried in vain to persuade him to tell her plainly. He loved his mother, but could not bring himself to speak of this matter to her. She detested my style of dress" (Memoir, 44).

Sarah had made her wedding outfit in the reform style, and it marked her as eccentric and controversial every step of the way. In Calais a crowd of young boys pelted her with snowballs. Sarah made a point of recording the comments of a certain Mr Pike, who scolded these boys and commended Joel on his choice of spouse: "While preparing to leave town, Joel met Mr Pike, who asked him 'Who is that lady I saw with you in that pretty dress?' Joel said, 'She is my wife, now.' 'I congratulate you on your choice,' was the reply. 'You have married a noble, sensible woman. *Such* a dress is comfortable, and a protection to its wearer. The way women usually dress, they have no protection against the weather, a dog, a *man*, or anything else!'" (Memoir, 44). Of course, this passage in her memoir likely reveals as much about Sarah's concern with consolidating her image as a "noble, sensible woman" as it does about the actual events. Certainly, she is intent on justifying her unusual choice of dress to her children many years later.

Even decades afterward, Sarah's description of the early days of her marriage in her memoir (which she subtitled "Romantic Reality") is shot through with rosy idealism: "Our ideas of 'Home,' beyond love and loyalty to each other, with righteousness and purity of life, were very simple and primitive. A shelter where we could be together, a bed and board, simply supplied, books and writing – the mediums of intercourse with the world of mind and letters – made home for us. We certainly appreciated, and could have enjoyed a more plentiful supply of the good things of life; but they were *not necessary to our happiness*" (Memoir, 45).

At first the most tempestuous relationship was with her aunt and mother-in-law, Martha Craig. After a winter of trying to make a living at a shingle mill on shares, Joel and Sarah were forced to admit failure and move into the house that Joel had shared with his mother. Mrs Craig was away at the time, but came home "looking like a thunder cloud" (Memoir, 46). Writing later in her memoir, Sarah is able to see this relationship in perspective:

> When Joel told her of the plan to build a cabin, and asked her to let me stay in her house till it was built, she advised him not to think of it, but get some land ready for crop; the house was big enough, etc. He was quite willing to be advised; for he could not have built any kind of a hut fit to live in without money or team, in time to do any farming. His mother now began to treat me a *little* more like a daughter, having apparently accepted the inevitable. She never learned to *like* my dress, which I then wore in a severely radical form; but evidently decided to make the best of it. She would often scold me like a naughty child; but by degrees we became good friends and might have been sooner, had I had the grace or tact to be *sweet* when she was sour or bitter; but I had not. (46)

Since Joel's mother was often away for weeks or months at a time, visiting relatives on Deer Island or even as far away as Eastport, Maine, Joel and Sarah often had the house to themselves.

Relationships with people in the community also continued to be a challenge for Sarah because of her style of dress. On one occasion during that first summer after their marriage, Joel's mother asked her to take a pail of fresh raspberries to her friend Ann Johnson, saying, "I guess she won't turn you out doors because you wear trousers!" (Memoir, 46). Surprisingly enough, Sarah's friendship with this woman, whom she came to call "Aunt Ann," became a valuable asset in a community which always viewed her with suspicion: "She did *not* like my 'trousers' at first, but she did like *me*; and so far from putting me out doors or ridiculing me, it was not very long before she 'took up the cudgels' in defence of my costume, and my independence in wearing it. Learning my reasons, she saw they were sound and logical; and often she said to me 'you have all the credit there is going'; meaning my dress had true principle at its back; because it answered the real purpose of dress, while fashionable attire did not. Dear Aunt Ann!" (Memoir, 46–7).

Sarah's insistence on wearing the reform dress full-time only served to entrench the differences between her and her community. Ironically, it also set her apart from many of the reformers she was trying to emulate. After the first wave of fervour inspired by Amelia Bloomer's wearing of her costume in 1851, many dress reformers of note abandoned it. Bloomer herself only wore the outfit for eight years.[46] True, there were women such as Mary Walker, a graduate in hydropathy at Trall's New York Hygeio-Therapeutic College, and the leading dress reformer, Harriet Austin, who wore some version of the reform dress for many years.[47] Ellen Beard Harman, who later lived and practised in Kokomo, Indiana, and Susan Pecker Fowler and Mary E. Tillotson of Vineland, New Jersey, also persisted in wearing the American Costume long after the movement had run out of steam. In an editorial in her magazine *Sibyl* entitled "The 'Principle' of Dress Reform," Lydia Sayer Hasbrouck railed at those notable women who had abandoned the battlefield of dress reform "at the first onset of the foe."[48] But women who, like her, continued wearing the outfit were definitely in the minority. Frontier women were especially likely to adopt the practical reform costume, which allowed much more freedom of movement for working outdoors in rough terrain. But most who wore the reform dress did so only at home when engaged in farm work, donning their more fashionable long dresses when they went out in public.[49] Dress historian Joan Severa notes that "only about a hundred women of note are known to have worn the costume, and most of those gave it up in the fifties because they deemed it injurious to their higher cause of women's rights because of its controversial nature. It was too distracting."[50]

By the 1860s even some prominent hydropaths had modified their stance on the reform dress. In an article in an 1862 issue of the *Water-Cure Journal*, an anonymous woman who signed herself "One who wears it" argued that the cause was actually being damaged by those who insisted that the costume be worn all the time. The writer says that

> we make a sad mistake ... in advocating it for others and teaching them that they were violating law if they put the dress on and took it off for any purpose. I have known women – good, conscientious women – who would not put the dress on just for this reason. They did not feel able to wear it all the time, and had been taught that it was wrong to leave it off after they once put it on. Some of our good sisters have also been very intolerant toward those who have found the persecution too great for them to bear, and have left off wearing it in public ... We can encourage all who feel inclined to wear it on any or all occasions, thus making it easier for them to do so.[51]

Another anonymous writer (perhaps Trall himself), in a piece entitled "The Dress Question," which appeared in the *Water-Cure Journal* in July 1862, argued that the radical nature of the costume

condemned dress reformers to "social outlawry."[52] For these reasons, the outfit was never broadly accepted among women.[53]
Those who wore it day in and day out, as their only style of dress,
were apparently quite rare. Sarah Craig probably did not know
that this was the case, since she lived far away from the centres of
action in New York and Boston. Or perhaps she did not care; once
convinced of the rightness of the cause, she was not prepared to
abandon it. In any case, she apparently continued to wear her
reform outfits for many years, becoming for some time a virtual
recluse on her farm to avoid the stares and distracting comments
of people at church and on the road. And near the end of her life,
when a neighbour woman put on her absent soldier son's pants
to pick fruit in her orchard, Sarah delightedly recalled her bygone
years as a dress reformer and quickly made herself a pair of
trousers to wear as well (Later diaries, 1917–18).

There is, however, the possibility, strongly implied in many of
Sarah's comments, that for her the reform dress was more than
just a practical form of clothing; that, like Lydia Sayer Hasbrouck,
Harriet Austin, Mary E. Tillotson, and other vocal female reformers, she saw fashionable women's clothing as "a continuing symbol
of woman's subservient position in American [and, by extension,
Canadian] society."[54] Certainly, the early advocate of women's
equality Elizabeth Cady Stanton, who was a friend of Amelia
Bloomer, explicitly linked women's dress reform with female
emancipation in her "Declaration of Sentiments," issued at an 1848
conference at Seneca Falls, New York.[55] In the pages of the *Sibyl*,
readers were told that woman would continue being dependent
"until she could by her own efforts prove to be self reliant and self
supporting which she could never do with her present style of
dress."[56] In her life writing, Sarah Craig constructs her relation-

ship with Joel as one of equality, at least as it would have been perceived in nineteenth-century terms. For instance, she records that
in April 1868, when Joel was pressured to sell his mill to clear a
debt, she exercised her "right of veto" as wife of the owner over
what she considered a bad deal, enabling him to work out a better
bargain. Her interest in this incident serves to consolidate her
image as an equal partner in the union, able to exercise her own
judgment in home affairs (Memoir, 74). She presents her function
as mother and housewife as only part of her persona (although a
very important part), and her descriptions of her pivotal role in
the colony scheme underscore her presentation of herself as an
equal partner in this marriage of minds. Thus she may well have
seen the restrictions of the corset and long skirt as symbolic of the
confinement of female intellect. Certainly, her use of words such
as "hampering," "fettering," and "thraldom" in her descriptions of
fashionable dress in her memoir suggests this subtext.

Of course, in an era when birth control was almost impossible
to obtain or ineffective, and when a married woman faced the
prospect of repeated pregnancies and births, the reform dress
was a comfortable and practical style of clothing that would not
restrict the development of the fetus in the womb as corsets
inevitably did. Indeed, health reformers railed at the fashionable
women who would not abandon their corsets during pregnancy
and who suffered as a result. The effects of corsets on the female
reproductive system could be severe; particularly horrifying was
the prolapsed uterus, "a condition in which the uterus is forced
through, or collapses outside of, the cervix, protrudes into the
vagina, and extreme cases, outside the body."[57] The treatments for
this condition – including the insertion of a device called a pessary
to push the uterus back up into its proper place – only exacerbated

the problem by increasing the pressure on the internal organs.[58] In an early volume of the *Water-Cure Journal* Mary Gove Nichols related several cases of women's disorders among her patients, including one of premature delivery, which she blamed on corsets.[59] Rachel Gleason warned her female readers of *prolapsus uteri* in her 1851 article on the evils of fashionable women's clothing, and other dress reformers joined her in recommending a more reasonable style of dress.[60] In 1883 Alice Stockham, who was both a doctor and a dress reformer, warned that corsets threatened the well-being of both mother and fetus and were "the chief cause of infantile mortality."[61] As late as 1900, J.H. Kellogg joined the chorus of voices against wearing corsets during pregnancy in his *Ladies' Guide in Health and Disease*.[62] However, as long as social taboos around the public display of the pregnant female body prevailed, most women remained determined to conceal their pregnancies as long as possible, and they could do so only by wearing corsets.[63]

Sarah Craig was certainly not among those women who valued fashion above comfort and safety. In the winter of 1861–62 she and Joel organized "a Society for Mutual Improvement; and especially for the study of Physiology, Hygiene, and the 'True Healing Art' and whatever betters and uplifts humanity" (Memoir, 49). Dubbed the Universal Progressive Reform Association, the group included Sarah's brothers Isaac and Henry, her sister, Martha, and a handful of sympathetic friends and neighbours. The members signed a series of pledges – nine in all – promising to abstain from alcohol and tobacco, from tea, coffee, salt, and meat, and from using alcohol or drugs in the treatment of disease; they also pledged to encourage and support the wearing of the reform dress by the women members, and to do all they could "to secure to Woman her Political, Social and Domestic Rights, which we believe to be identical with those of men" (it is interesting that only three of the men signed this last pledge!).[64] It seems that, aside from the study of health reform, one of the group's main functions was to provide a refuge from the hostility of the community at large. Sarah writes:

> Opposition to our peculiar ideas and manner of life had been growing more outspoken and offensive. Not that we paraded or intruded our views upon others; we were not *permitted to be quiet*. Certain parties *would* talk and draw us out, then argue, or try to, and oppose; while we were bound to defend what we knew to be right. Quite a few of the opposers, after examining the groundwork of the reforms we advocated, began to see that they were necessary and important; and seeking more light, heartily joined with us in our studies. We were much handicapped by lack of reading matter at that time, but made the most of what we had among us; adding a little to our stock as we could. We managed to keep up our subscription to the "Herald of Health," and "Laws of Life" and reading, and occasionally writing for these Journals, kept us in touch of the vanguard of the principal reforms of that day. (Memoir, 49)

The hydropathic lifestyle was certainly radically different from the "normal" nineteenth-century way of life in many ways. If one were fortunate, sickness struck only occasionally; but the rules governing diet and hygiene were a daily matter. Dietary habits were likely to be perceived as especially queer because of their strictness; after all, even salt was prohibited. Not only were there regulations about which foods should be eaten and which avoided, but the timing and size of meals was also strictly regimented. Sarah's "Letter from Auntie," published in the August 1864 issue of the *Herald of Health*, in the magazine's children's section, gives a detailed glimpse of the health-reform life. Little Edwin, the child addressee (and, not coincidentally, the name of Sarah's youngest brother), is advised not to eat "one mouthful of anything between meals, not even berries, nuts, or anything else ... Never touch pork, in any form or shape, or any thing in any way pertaining to it, or fine flour pie crust, shortened with lard, or pickles, preserves, rich cake or candies. Avoid fine flour fermented bread, always, when by any possibility you can procure any other. If you eat meat, use only fresh beef, mutton, and the like, and of that partake very sparingly during warm weather. Live mainly upon unleavened Graham bread, fruits, fresh vegetables, etc."

Little Edwin is counselled not to "eat too much," especially in summer, since "every mouthful too much is a clog, a course of disease, taxing the energies of the system to get rid of it." And he is to be wary of playing too hard. Little Edwin replies, thanking Auntie for her good advice, and expressing the following unchildlike sentiments: "I was always brought up to eating three meals a day, until last November, when I went to live with my married sister, who, with her husband and his mother, ate but two meals a day, and I joined them ... I think when I grow up, I shall live upon a vegetarian diet exclusively, and be a practical hygienist. I intend to totally abstain from all intoxicating beverages, tea, coffee, or tobacco in any form; and use my influence against the use of such."[65] This didactic little passage is typical in style of the "kindergarten department" of the journal. The dietary regimen described by Little Edwin is virtually identical to that followed at Jackson's Our

Home on the Hillside, and one clearly followed by Sarah Craig (the "married sister" mentioned by Little Edwin) and her husband and mother-in-law. The diet was obviously influenced by the system promoted by Sylvester Graham, with his emphasis on abstinence from alcohol and tobacco, vegetarianism, and moderation in eating.[66] Although it appears that there were times when Joel and Sarah did eat meat when they had no other food (such as the occasion when one of their sheep drowned in the lake), they were generally so poor that a vegetarian diet was their only option.

The Reform Association's first major test came in the spring of 1862, when Sarah's oldest brother, Albert, the shipbuilder, came home, desperately ill, from Cleveland, where he had been working. The diagnosis was "consumption," or tuberculosis. His friends there were sure he had gone home to die, but Albert knew that his sister and his mother had studied the water-cure system, and he put himself under their care.

> He bought a treatise on Consumption, by Dr Jackson, head physician of "Our Home on the Hillside," Dansville, NY; and began to study and practice at once, with mother as doctor and nurse, and myself in frequent consultation; going deeper as he learned more of Hygiene in diet, bathing, and bodily habits; but giving special attention to the special needs of his own case. Having saved a few hundred dollars, besides all he had sent home from time to time, he was able to provide himself with such extras as he needed – packing sheets, towels, etc., and the best wheat meal, then $4.00 per hundred pounds! He had the wheat bought *whole*, to be sure it was best quality and *clean*; and ground in McAllister's Mill at

Salmon Falls or Milltown. For fruit there were wild berries a plenty. (Memoir, 50)

By the autumn of 1862 Albert's health had greatly improved. As winter neared, he decided that his family's draughty cabin might prove dangerous to his delicate health, and so he set off for New York to put himself under treatment at R.T. Trall's Hygienic Institute, which operated as a clinic as well as a training and publishing centre for the hydropathy movement. Sarah declares that "within three months he was cured, and working at his trade in New York Dock Yards" (Memoir, 50). She notes triumphantly, "Albert's complete recovery under the new system was a great surprise to all his and our friends, and a triumph for the cause in our neighborhood; as few if any but ourselves believed when he came home, that he could recover. And he certainly *could* not have survived a course of drug treatment" (Memoir, 51).

The twenty-first-century reader knows, of course, that tuberculosis is caused by a bacterium and could never be cured simply through diet and applications of water to the body. Even Trall himself admitted in his *Hydropathic Encyclopedia* that advanced cases of tubercular consumption were almost always fatal. He maintained, however, that if caught early enough, the disease could be treated through a rigorous vegetarian diet, exercise in fresh air, and the drinking of five to ten tumblers of pure water per day, along with frequent baths of various types.[67] This was almost certainly the treatment followed by Albert Jameson. Whether his recovery had anything to do with this treatment or was simply a matter of rest, better nutrition, and good luck will never be known.

Sarah claims that a few neighbours were heard to mutter, "If that kind of doctoring cures an incurable, there must be *something* in it!" (Memoir, 51). Yet there is little evidence in her memoir or diaries that this event resulted in any permanent improvement in the way that she and her family were generally perceived. Instead, she depicts a community consistently hostile toward her and her views. Sarah's diaries and reminiscences often reveal an intense sense of isolation. At one point she writes, "The people among whom we lived were mostly slow, ignorant, stolid; living in a rut; never thinking (or if told never believing) there was any other or better way to live. Many were intensely low-lived, vulgar, and pro-fane ... I am glad to say that there were many noble exceptions – good, intelligent, reading and thinking Christians; but they were too conservative to sympathize with our ultra ideas ... we had scarcely *one* congenial spirit, with whom we could talk face to face" (Memoir, 58). Even her own father was, if not overtly hos-tile, hardly sympathetic; when Albert sent home a carton of books given to him in payment for work he had done while staying at Dr Trall's institute, "Father saw the initials, 'U.P.R.A.' [Universal Pro-gressive Reform Association], partly got hold of the name, and dubbed it the 'Un-Principled Rowdy Association,' enjoying many a laugh over it at his own wit, at our expense, he thought; but his fun never hurt, only amused us; we could afford to let him have his joke, while we fed our minds on the rich stores of knowledge now within our reach" (Memoir, 50–1).

Sarah and Joel had other matters on their minds at this time as well: their first living child was born on 10 November 1862 (their first baby had apparently been stillborn about a year before). The infant boy, Jimmy, was fretful at first, but when Joel's mother came

home from a visit to Deer Island and undertook to instruct Sarah
in the care of infants ("her advice came mostly as scoldings," remarks Sarah wryly in her memoir), he began to thrive. All apparently went well until Mrs Craig went away again at Christmas and
Sarah was left in the house with the baby and all the daily work
besides. While Mrs Craig was in Eastport, Maine, she had "a dream
that seemed a warning of death and turned her face homeward"
(Memoir, 52). Sarah's heart-wrenching account of what happened
is included in her memoir:

> Friday night we retired late and very weary. I had made baby
> a pair of rabbit skin stockings to wear to mother's on Sunday,
> and could hardly keep my eyes open. I put baby to my breast,
> but must have gone at once to sleep myself, instead of wait-
> ing to lift his head to the pillow as usual, where he could
> breathe freely. In the night I awoke, and missing his little
> head, cried out, "Where's baby?," waking Joel, and fearing – I
> knew not what. In a few moments I found him, down under
> my arm and breast, quite still – *too* still. I quickly drew him
> to the pillow, while Joel lit a lamp; to our horror we found he
> was dead – smothered! His tiny limbs even then were stiffen-
> ing! Frantically we tried to resuscitate him by artificial
> breathing, working over him for nearly an hour; but in vain –
> all in vain! The dear little life had gone out "as one bloweth
> out a candle"!
>
> Of the remainder of that fearful night, I cannot write.
> Only one awful fact stood out clearly; our lovely, precious
> boy, so healthy, bright and winning a few brief hours ago,
> had been suddenly snatched away, by Death's resistless hand.
> Only the previous morning, he had laughed his first audible
> little laugh, when I kissed his tiny palm! (52)

Mrs Craig arrived home, fearing that it was her own son, Joel, who had died, but finding instead that her little grandson, of whom she had quickly become very fond, was the one who had been taken. Sarah writes that "it seemed that the sun had gone out of the sky" (Memoir, 52), and she had to return to her daily household routine with a desolate heart.

The Hygienic Institute, or New York Hygeio-Therapeutic College, as it was later called, run by R.T. Trall, offered a diploma in hydropathy. In 1857 the college had been granted a New York State charter, which enabled it to grant an MD degree – much to the horror of regular physicians, who saw this development as a victory for "quackery."[68] The course consisted of twenty weeks of lectures at $1.00 per lecture; on completing it, the student was issued a diploma for $30.00. Both men and women were accepted into the course, a significant inducement in an era when women were rarely admitted to conventional American medical schools. Trall and other hydropaths actively encouraged women to apply to study hydropathy, and indeed many of the students at the college were female.[69]

Sarah and Joel, ever on the lookout for a way to escape their poverty, longed to take the course and qualify as hydropathic physicians. In 1863 the possibility seemed to offer itself:

Joel and I had been eagerly looking and wishing – hardly hoping – for a way to open for one of us to attend a course of lectures at the Hygienic College at 15 Laight Street, and qualify as a physician. Dr Trall was sending out capable men and women physicians from every graduating class; but could not supply the demand. A single course, with our previous studies, would have fitted either of us for the Diploma and MD. But how? Now Albert, baching in New York, near the College,

seemed to offer a chance for me to go and keep house for my
board, and attend the lectures, if I could arrange with the
Doctor. I wrote to him, and he readily offered to credit me
with matriculation fees and the price of the course, confident
that I could soon pay it upon graduating. (Memoir, 52)

By 1869 the college would be offering a few free scholarships to
needy students, a provision that was made clear in advertisements
for the course, such as the one on the back cover of the October
1869 issue of the *Phrenological Journal and Life Illustrated*. However, it seems that this practice had not yet been instituted in 1863,
and so Sarah would have had to repay the tuition fees. Unfortunately, a tragic event conspired with her overly rigid principles to
thwart her plans.

Albert sent me $20.00 to fit me out and pay my fare; but in-
sisted that I must wear a long dress and crinoline (hoops!) in
the fashionable way! Though he partly understood, and believed in, the principles of Dress Reform, he was not radical
enough to stand by his sister in a costume that would fling
revolt right in the teeth of fashionable New York.
    It did not take us long to decide in the negative, which
was most fortunate; for as it proved, any other course would
have been disastrous. I wrote thanking him, but saying I
could not accept the money on such conditions. (Memoir,
52–3)

In fact, Albert had been killed in a construction accident a few
days before Sarah wrote her answering letter, and on receiving the

news of his death, the whole family was plunged into an intense
period of mourning. Albert's wages had been an important extra
source of income for the family, and of course his death meant
that there was nobody to keep house for in New York. Sarah writes
that when she heard the news, it became "plain ... why I was prov-
identially withheld from going to New York" (Memoir, 53). This
wording obscures the issue; she was not "withheld" from going,
but chose not to go because of her principles concerning dress. In
fact, on what turned out to be the day of his death, Albert's letter
containing the promised $20.00 arrived. Sarah probably could
have used the money for passage to New York, stayed at the institute, earned her diploma, and paid the school back, if she had chosen to do so.

There may have been another consideration holding her back,
however: she was almost certainly pregnant at the time with her
third child, Albert, who was born on 31 December 1863 (Memoir,
54–5). If she knew of the pregnancy at the time of her brother's
offer, she would have had an added incentive to avoid wearing the
conventional corseted dress for fear of harming her unborn child.
Having only recently lost their second baby, Jimmy, she and Joel
would have been determined to take every measure possible to
avoid any risks to this third pregnancy.

If, on the other hand, she did not know she was pregnant at
the time, Sarah's refusal to wear conventional dress, even temporarily and in furtherance of her noble goals, underlines her im-
movability in matters of principle, a rigidity that often seems (to
the reader) to be abject foolishness. An MD from the Hygienic College would have opened doors to a whole new life for her and Joel
– not necessarily one of magnificent wealth, but at least one lived

above the poverty line. Their refusal to bend an inch on the dress issue meant that a potentially viable career path was closed to both of them.

Instead of using Albert's money to go to New York, Sarah and Joel invested it in "a stock of small wares for sale; thread, needles, pins, buttons in variety, pens, paper, and notions; – articles that would sell at sight at good profits, yet were not too bulky or heavy to carry from house to house" (Memoir, 54). Joel became a peddler and limped his way from house to house throughout the rural community. This trade brought in some small income, but it was never really enough, and they were often dependent upon the generosity of Sarah's family or neighbours. Her chronicle of the next two years is one of constant economic struggle and privation, with Joel continuing his peddling and Sarah selling butter and eggs in St Stephen, miles away. As she describes their situation in her memoir, "We were regarded by many as the *beggars* of the community; albeit very intelligent, good-natured beggars, handy to have about when services of *brain* or *mechanics' tools* were required. Those who thus looked down upon us, being above *want* – (so-called) – themselves, were not above begging the use of our brains or 'borrowing' husband's tools; *always* returning the latter dulled, bent, broken, or in some way abused" (60). Sarah and Joel were often on the brink of starvation. There had to be a better way of life.

Chapter Two

A Colony of Reformers

> I may not be able to make clear to my readers all that this idea
> and the project meant to many of us; but for a few years it was
> the earthly goal to which we looked forward, and for which we
> lived and worked. (Memoir, 57)

So wrote Sarah Craig in her later years as she constructed her personal "History" for her children. This "earthly goal" was a utopian scheme to establish a self-sufficient colony of Christian health and dress reformers, a community of people with similar intellectual and spiritual interests dedicated to the "enlightened education" of both male and female members. This project proved to be both the most exciting and the most frustrating one of her life.

In 1864 Joel and Sarah launched their plan to organize a "Colony of Reformers." Such a community would be a communal farm, run along strict principles of religion and "progressive health reform." Sarah explains in her memoir that the idea had been taking shape for some time, but was dependent on a number of "ifs":

> If we can find a number – the more the better – of intelligent,
> progressive men and women (*Christian reformers*) to join us
> in settling somewhere on Uncle Sam's free Homestead lands,

blessed with fertile soil, mild climate; a prairie country, with
some timber and plenty of water, etc., what a delightful
community of homes could be made, as a nucleus of future
developments! And how much *easier* we could live pure, natural, simple lives, studying and obeying God's laws in nature;
helping and encouraging each other; than we can scattered,
isolated, surrounded by opposition and "various hindrances,"
as we now are. (57)

The Craigs' thinking on these matters was likely influenced by
Harriet Austin's article "An Extraordinary Community" in the
March 1860 issue of the *Water-Cure Journal*. Here Austin describes
a utopia that resembles in many ways the one proposed by Joel
and Sarah. Her ideal community of "about a thousand souls"
would include "a saw-mill, a paper-mill, a grist-mill, a printing-
office, a shoe shop, a sewing and knitting room," and all other
mechanized functions to make the community self-sufficient.
Families would each have their own cottage, but meals would be
communal and everyone would eat together in a large central
house with a dining room that was spacious enough to accom-
modate everyone. In this vegetarian utopia, people would maintain their health and beauty into old age and would never die of
disease. Austin's lovingly drawn picture of a harmonious reform
colony must have worked powerfully on the Craigs' imaginations.

Their determination to settle "somewhere on Uncle Sam's free
Homestead lands" was probably also inspired by their reading of
the *Water-Cure Journal*. The 1862 issues carried numerous advertisements for land available in the West. Moreover, in the February 1862 issue R.T. Trall himself published an article entitled
"Rambling Reminiscences #6: Our Trip to the West," in which he
described his impressions of the potential for settlement there.

Thus, although they had never travelled west of Calais, Maine, Joel and Sarah had a picture in their minds of what the west was like and its advantages – chief of which was free arable land – for reformers like them.

In an article published in the January 1864 issue of the *Herald of Health* (the successor to the *Water-Cure Journal*), Joel set forth their goal as follows:

> We have resolved to form a colony of true, Christian, dress, and health reformers, in some new, retired, fertile, and healthful district, where there is an abundance of pure soft water, (and water-power for driving machinery) and a fair growth of light timber, for building and other purposes; where we may "worship God in our bodies as well as our spirits," free from the frowns, persecutions, and evil influences of fashionable society; where those who wish to reform their habits of life, but have not strength and resistance sufficient to overcome the opposition of those by whom they are now surrounded, may find a home in which they can grow and enjoy the company and counsel of pure and congenial spirits; where profanity, licentiousness, and quarreling shall not be tolerated, and where the manufacture, sale and use of all alcoholic and drug medicines shall be forever prohibited (except perhaps in some rare surgical cases); where foul tobacco shall not be allowed in any form, and where innocent animals shall not be abused, killed, and devoured by human beings as in other places.[1]

The article goes on to describe a community in which the sexes would be equal, boys and girls would be educated together, and education would be free to all. Those interested in joining such a colony are urged to write to J.B. Craig, president of the Universal Progressive Reform Association.

Many of the principles articulated here were standard for the health-reform movement. The banning of tobacco and alcoholic drug medications was a central tenet of the water-cure system. Also common, although not universal, was the emphasis on vegetarianism; in fact, many of the leaders of the water-cure movement in the United States, including Trall, were vegetarians, much influenced by Sylvester Graham's system.[2] Although it is clear from Sarah's writings that she and Joel did sometimes eat meat, their diet was usually from necessity a vegetarian one. The emphasis on the equality of boys and girls, especially in education, is another central theme in the water-cure movement, although very few of the established communities lived up to this stated goal, and women still tended to suffer from stereotyping.[3]

Perhaps most importantly, the colony idea reflects the hydropathic emphasis on a whole new approach to life in general and not simply to sickness. As Cayleff puts it, hydropathy "stressed a comprehensive approach to disease management that left no aspect of life unregulated."[4] Thus it was perhaps only natural that some of its followers would seek to separate themselves from nonbelievers in order to form their own congenial society. The *Water-Cure Journal* and its successor, the *Herald of Health*, even carried personal advertisements that allowed subscribers to search for like-minded mates. The colony proposed by Sarah and Joel was simply an extension of this idea of creating "family" among water-cure adherents.

The longing for freedom from opposition is also central to Joel's call for a separate community. In the preamble to his colony article he devotes much space to lamenting the hostile climate in which health reformers had to live:

> Situated as the majority of reformers now are, it is impossible for them to attain to anything like perfection. Vice, misery, and crime; intemperance, profanity, licentiousness; tobacco-using, with all its accompanying evils; brutality, and the devouring of murdered animals; with the worse than barbarous drug medical system, are anything but favorable surroundings for those who would "present their bodies as living sacrifices, holy and acceptable to God"; and "train up their children in the nurture and admonition of the Lord" ... How are we to "train up a child in the way he (or she) should go," when the whole community is busily engaged in poisoning the atmosphere with tobacco and other deadly poisons; and laying every possible snare to entangle its unsuspecting mind in the ways of unrighteousness?[5]

This is obviously a description of the Craigs' own community as they perceived it. The underlying assumption is that other readers of the *Herald of Health* were living in similar circumstances and would also be eager to separate themselves from their ignorant neighbours. Joel's reference to attaining "perfection" fits in with the ideas about the perfectibility of humankind that characterized this era. The mixing of biblical quotations with the language of health reform is typical of how closely the two belief systems were aligned in the minds of many reformers. In fact, in much of the health-reform literature there is a constant linking of fashion, unhealthful diet, and drug medication with biblical notions of "worldliness" and "sinfulness" and an implicit identification of the reformers with the "people of God."

The Craigs' perception of their cause as "righteous" was no doubt partly responsible for the hostility they faced from some of their neighbours. Just as the dress reformers' distinct tone of self-righteousness eventually contributed to the failure of the movement to garner broad support among women's rights advocates, so too did the Craigs' insistence on the superiority of their healing practices alienate them from their own community, although their unorthodox methods of healing did not help. The apparently miraculous recovery of Sarah's brother Albert from consumption under the new methods clearly impressed the community, but it did little to reconcile its members to Sarah and Joel's radical ideas about diet and their practice of water cure. Indeed, Sarah's two accounts (one in her memoir, the other in a letter published in the *Herald of Health* in August 1864) of her treatment of a pregnant woman who had collapsed on the road and was temporarily paralyzed highlight the hostile response of the community to her methods. The letter to the *Herald of Health* focuses more precisely on the techniques of doctoring that she used, since these would interest the readership of adherents to the water-cure system. Sarah writes of her imposition of a strict diet of "fresh oatmeal gruel, apples, oranges, raisins ... and Graham bread when she could take it," instead of the meat, fine salted bread, and draughts of gin that the woman's relatives favoured. There is a note of triumph in her comment that "they only managed to give her salted gruel twice when we were not on hand."[6]

In her memoir Sarah dispenses with the specific details about doctoring and focuses on the opposition that she and her partners in care (her mother and sister) faced from the young woman's family:

At evening as Mary Ann Smith and I stood by the door, apart, she asked me, with tearful eyes if I thot Jemima would get well. There seemed no sign of it; she had grown weaker all day, and it put my faith in God, Nature and hygiene to a severe test, to say I believed she would. But I did say it, and my faith was not put to shame. The one thing we could not do was to keep her quiet. House all one room, without chamber (just a quilt curtain around the bed) and half a score or more of callers coming and going all day – talking, talking incessantly and often loud, but in condemnation of our plan of treatment *and the patient could hear it all!* The crowd left at night and we worked in peace. At eleven p.m. I wrung again the flannel (kept in hot water on the stove) and changed the fomentation, and presently the patient's last pain vanished and she slept sweetly. So did we all. In the morning she was very much better, and gained rapidly. But her father, whose pet and darling she was, refused to believe it as long as possible; and it actually seemed that he would rather she had died, than recovered under "such crazy doctoring." But she is living yet. (56)

In fact, Jemima was the wife of Sarah's oldest brother, Isaac, who later led his family west and joined several unsuccessful utopian colonies. In a passage included in the handwritten version of Sarah's memoir, but for some reason not reproduced in Florence's typescript, Sarah reveals that this episode occurred just after Jemima had given birth to her first baby, which was born with a malformed skull. The infant lived only a week, and Jemima was stricken with severe pain and fever. The true nature of her illness remains unclear in all of Sarah's accounts; whatever it was, the hydropathic treatment that Sarah offered apparently helped to at least ease her symptoms. And indeed, Jemima had several other children and lived to a ripe old age, dying in 1915.

Yet this incident apparently provoked much anger in the community. Sarah's account in her letter to the *Herald of Health* is evangelical in tone and may well be exaggerated, yet it perhaps affords a glimpse of the prevailing mood:

> Our treatment of this case brought down the wordy vengeance of the whole neighbourhood, and all the neighbourhoods around, on our heads. The most scandalous falsehoods about "starving," "freezing," "drowning," etc., were circulated for miles around. Her father came and "raised a breeze" about her food and treatment; but neither threats, persuasion, ridicule, nor the grossest misrepresentation could move us from our allegiance to the better way. Any one with less faith in Nature and Hygiene than her husband (my brother) and myself would have faltered, but we held true to our principles and succeeded.[7]

The accusation of "starving" here refers to the water-cure practice of drastically reducing food intake during illness. Sarah was following the recommendations given in articles such as "Eating When Sick," in which a hydropathic doctor claims that "nine-tenths of the acute diseases might be prevented by a few days' starvation," which he defines as "perhaps a piece of cold bread, with cold water for drink."[8] From Sarah's account, it is clear that Jemima was fed more than this bare minimum, but the principle of withholding food in order to avoid "exhausting" the stomach was undoubtedly perplexing to the average person.

Sarah's zeal for the water-cure system and the problems it caused her are evident in her account. Whether or not the community was as hostile as she says, her *perception* of its hostility is clear. Nor is the depiction of such opposition unusual in accounts published in the *Herald of Health* and other reform-movement publications. Their editors indulged in often vitriolic condemnations of the methods of traditional allopathic (conventional) medicine, and they described the "conversion" of allopathic physicians to the water-cure ideology in terms very similar to those used of religious conversion. The *Herald of Health* encouraged readers to write in with reports of successful cures, and the pages were often filled with the readers' own "triumphs" with water cure in the face of strong resistance from family members. As a result, the tone used in accounts of hydropathic healing was often evangelical, and the line between "right" and "wrong" methods was sharply delineated.

In the context of such perceived opposition from the community, the idea of a colony of kindred spirits, living far from the derisive eyes of such ignorant neighbours, must have seemed akin to paradise. In fact, the concept of a health-reform community of "congenial minds" was not a new one. Temporary versions of such communities already existed at the many water-cure establishments scattered around New York and in other states. At these institutions, patients were temporarily removed from "hostile society," and women staying at these centres could wear their reform dresses without provoking negative remarks and could get to know other, like-minded individuals. A sense of nostalgia for good times together at these water-cure establishments pervades early issues of the *Letter Box*, the newsletter of Dr Jackson's Our

Home on the Hillside in Dansville, New York.[9] Unfortunately, since only people of certain means could afford to stay at these places, they were in effect open solely to members of the prosperous middle and upper classes. Such communities, then, were not available to Sarah and Joel Craig, nor to the large number of other people who practised hydropathy at home.

The call for a "Colony of Reformers" in the *Herald of Health* brought a deluge of correspondence from eager health and dress reformers all across North America; as Sarah puts it in her memoir, "The spark caught, kindled and blazed far and wide, East, West and South," from as far away as California (57). Most correspondents lived in the United States, but some letters came from Canada East and West, as Quebec and Ontario were then known. Sarah and Joel had to add secretarial duties to their daily struggle for survival: "All our spare time and much of our sleeping time was spent writing and answering letters. Forwarding and receiving our mail through Calais post office, we used the US 3-cent stamps, which were freely furnished by our correspondents ... When our neighbours went to town they usually crossed the river and by them we sent our letters – often 12 to 16 at a time – and a line to the Postmaster would bring our mail back" (Memoir, 57).

The amount of correspondence soon became a great burden. Surviving letters to some neighbours who had moved away after joining the UPRA suggest that each of these was often more than two handwritten pages in length. Sarah was answering letters with her month-old baby Albert on her lap. To a large extent, each correspondent required the same basic information, written over and over again. This problem gave rise to the idea of acquiring a small printing press. Sarah and Joel imagined that a press would allow them to print leaflets and perhaps even a "tiny periodical." They wrote to their correspondents, who immediately began sending small amounts of money for a press – from twenty-five cents to a dollar each. The Craigs acquired some type at no cost when American raiders attacked the *St Croix Herald* office in St Stephen at night and threw the printing equipment into the river. Joel and Sarah's brother Isaac found it there early the next morning and carried home "two quarts of pied type" (Memoir, 57). While waiting for enough money to purchase a press, one of the prospective colonists, Joseph Briscoe, had a batch of the group's constitution and pledges printed up while he was staying at Our Home on the Hill in Dansville (Memoir, 57). These were mailed out to the correspondents by Sarah and Joel.

When there was finally enough money to buy the press they wanted, however, disappointment set in:

Now, having the funds – which had been sent in little by little – we sent at once to Lowe Press Co., Boston, for their No. 3 roller job press and four fonts of type; three of minion, and one of fancy capitals for headings. This, with the old we had, we thought would print a double page 9 x 12, which size the press would print with larger chases. Joel made patterns, and Moses Craig, machinist and blacksmith at Salmon Falls, cast the chases, one with a border line and one without. Though we got the outfit early in the year, it was not till October, '64, that we struck the first number of "The Car of Progress" – a name full of meaning which we hoped to make the paper realize – and sent it on the wings of the mail. But the type, after all, could only be made to print the first and a part of the last pages – one side of sheet – first and last pages indeed! For we had learned, even then, that the work of conducting a paper,

even so small, without means or more facilities than we
could command, was utterly beyond us; and we were very reluctantly forced to admit the same, first to ourselves, then to
our friends. (Memoir, 58)

Once again limited resources had foiled Sarah and Joel's plans.
They nevertheless kept up the correspondence with would-be
colonists by hand, "still urging the cause along, and seeking our
Eden," as Sarah puts it (Memoir, 57).

In the meantime, letters from prospective colonists kept coming. Each of these new friends had his or her own idea of which
region would best meet the criteria for the colony's success as a
self-sufficient community:

About the first query in every letter was about the locality.
The Colony idea was good – was great; "but WHERE?" Some
of our correspondents who had travelled a bit, thought they
had seen the right place, and enlarged on the natural advantages it possessed; others claimed the region round their own
home couldn't be beat; and so on. To get the minds of "all
and singular" involved much writing; then to sift the various
opinions, and make a wise decision, required a deal of work,
and was a big responsibility. (Memoir, 57)

Joel's initial article had expressed the hope of taking advantage of
the Homestead Law in the western United States, but this proved
impossible. Instead, land agents wrote only of property for sale,
at prices that most of the prospective colonists could not afford.
Sarah writes that one Minnesota company offered us "the refusal
of a township for $24,000. *We did not take it!*" (Memoir, 58). It be-

came increasingly clear that establishing a community of this sort would not be as easy as it had first appeared. The process of choosing a location continued for almost two years, during which time the correspondents began to grow impatient, "eager to get to the land of promise without more delay" (Memoir, 59).

Unfortunately, these efforts were disrupted and ultimately doomed by a disastrous house fire in January 1865. Sarah's one-year-old son, Albert, had become very ill with whooping cough. Having lost her first two babies, she was understandably determined to do all she could for him. She records in her diary: "Jan. 22nd. – Albert's cough is very severe, threatening to give him a tough time. Our house is so open and cold, I cannot give him proper baths, or even keep him comfortably warm half the time. So I have arranged to spend a few weeks with him at mother's. His papa does not favor the idea at all; but mother's folks do, and strongly advise it … Husband's mother is at home; but he is feeling quite unwell, and took my leaving *very* hard" (Early diaries). In fact, a letter from Joel to Sarah dated 9 March 1865 reveals that for some reason he thought Sarah had left him permanently and that he was extremely upset. They seem to have disagreed over the treatment of Albert's illness rather more vigorously than Sarah's diary account indicates. At any rate, their household was certainly disrupted, and Joel's distraction may have been partly responsible for the disaster that followed.

On 29 January, while both Joel and his mother were out, the house caught fire and burned to the ground. Sarah's diary entry captures her desolation:

Not only our poor, barn-like house is gone, with our clothing, bedding, furniture, provisions … and what little money

we had; but our noble and valuable library of books, magazines and periodicals – volumes of History, Biography, Trav-
els, Science, literature, art etc, for which with our piles of
manuscripts and correspondence, we would not have taken
any money, and which no money can restore – all, all "swept
to oblivion by one fell stroke of the relentless destroyer." With
the rest, of course, went the library and other property of the
UPRA – all except two books and a few tracts. The printing
press was ruined, types fused into a mass, correspondence,
and some money lost. (Early diaries)

Left destitute, Joel and Sarah were forced to focus all their energies
on their own survival. On receiving a new batch of letters from
prospective colonists and seeing that one contained $2.00, they
used the money for their own urgent needs. Later, as word of the
disaster spread, more help arrived. "When our Club friends heard
of our holocaust, those who could sent small sums of money for
our own use. It being always in postal currency, or 'green backs,'
was worth then 40 cents on the dollar – i.e. one dollar in U.S. paper
was worth 40 cents in cash" (Memoir, 62).

Friends and neighbours rallied round and donated wood and
other materials for a new log cabin, helping Joel when they could
with the building. For a time, the community that Sarah so reviles
in her diaries and memoir actually seems to have shown them extraordinary kindness. Slowly, through the generosity of these
friends and neighbours, the Craigs were able to finish at least the
shell of their new house and move in. Still, they had no beds at
first, and only enough shingles to cover half the roof to keep the
rain out. Food was scanty, and work was as hard to come by as
ever. Sarah sums up their privation thus:

We generally had clothes of some kind to cover us, and most days had *something* to eat. Sometimes, after we had pinched all we could from our stock of seed peas, beans corn, etc., to cook, tiding us over an extra bad place, and had enjoyed a respite by means of a bag of meal or other supply for a *Providential* bit of work, along came a fierce storm, just as the barrel was empty, – and no job meantime; – then we would get *so hungry*, I would bring out my little parcels of seed, and pinch out a few more handfuls – one from each lot, perhaps – and make a pot of delicious soup! (Memoir, 66)

Yet they had lost much more than the physical necessities of life. In fact, Sarah hints in her memoir that Joel may have descended into depression after this catastrophe: "I, in the meantime, had my hands full with the care of our boy; and being still 'daughter in my mother's house,' robust in health, scarcely knowing the meaning of 'nerves,' – though I *deeply* and sharply felt our terrible loss, it did not *strike in* so deeply, and was not such an agony of torture to me as to him. Baby must be cared for, being in a most critical condition" (Memoir, 62).

Unfortunately, as time went on, the kindness of neighbours slowly dropped off: "By this time [May 1865], many of the people around us far and near believed that we were as well fixed as before the fire. Little they knew of the preciousness of many of our lost treasures, poor and unsightly as some of them were; and still less would they have cared had they known. *Such* treasures – furniture and garniture for *soul* housekeeping – were not in their line. Believing we had had more given us than we could *possibly* have lost, the giving practically ceased; certainly the asking ceased" (Memoir, 64). Here again Sarah articulates the sense of alienation from her community that characterizes almost all of her writing about the New Brunswick years. The treasures she refers to are, of course, the many books, magazines, and pamphlets that she and Joel had collected over the years. Without these, they both felt truly bereft.

Shortly after the fire, Sarah wrote to the *Herald of Health* to inform correspondents whose addresses had been lost in the fire and to ask them to write again. For some reason, this first letter was never published. In October she wrote again; her letter appeared in the November 1865 issue. Her brave rhetoric and apparent determination mask the desperate situation at home:

> Our friends probably think we have grown lukewarm in the cause, and given up the "Colony" enterprise for want of means to carry it out. We wish to assure our friends that our zeal has not one whit abated, nor our determination grown weaker to seek and find a congenial home for ourselves, and all who can join hand, heart and soul with us – where we shall be wholly free from the trammels of society and fashionable life – free to live, and grow back into the arms of Mother Nature, and make our home an Eden! Though obstacles have seemed to thicken in our path, we confidently trust in God, firmly believing that He will aid all who earnestly labor for the establishment of His kingdom on earth.[10]

Responses began to arrive again in the mail. Some of the prospective colonists again sent small amounts of money for the family's relief. Many must have supplied postage stamps for return mail, because the Craigs rarely had even the few cents for stamps that letters required.

At last, in the spring of 1866, Sarah and Joel thought they had found the right location for their colony:

> Our friends had agreed that as we were the original movers of the "Colony Scheme," we should decide where we were to pitch the Colony tent. And we, after comparing, sifting, and weighing all the information we could secure, selected South-eastern Kansas, as more nearly realizing our ideal in soil, climate and other respects. Soon after we made known our choice of locality, William Sheldon, a young man who knew that region well, and had helped us make our decision, married and went there to reside. He wrote in glowing terms of the climate, crops, water, timber, wild fruits, etc.; and said that he and his wife one day climbed a wild grape-vine and gathered two bushels of luscious grapes. The very *thought* of grapes in such abundance was a great attraction, but only one of many. (Memoir, 58)

The Craigs wrote to the other prospective colonists and announced their choice. Of course, what they had selected was only a *region*; they still did not have a specific piece of land on which to build their colony. Sarah and Joel also lacked the financial resources to purchase land in the United States, and many of their correspondents were almost as poor as they were. "Some could sell their homes to good advantage; others with no homes to sell, wanted homes to keep; all wished to locate permanently. *We* were prevented from 'leading the tribes forward'; but others need not wait for us" (Memoir, 59).

Timing was a complicating factor in the Craigs' plans for the colony. The impact of the American Civil War on an area such as

southwestern New Brunswick, which was closely linked economically and socially to the United States, was significant. In 1866 the
American government cancelled the Reciprocity Treaty, and trade
with the British North American colonies was sharply curtailed.
That same year the Craigs sold fifty acres of their property to a
neighbour to clear a debt, for which they received only $100.00.
Even selling the entire property would not have yielded enough
cash for them to move south.

> Farm property, never high priced in our part of NB, was less
> saleable than ever, during the period of readjustment of fi-
> nances and reconstruction of State relations and conditions
> in the US incident on the closing of the war. Our place,
> therefore, would bring but a small price, if it sold at all. We
> could not go unless we sold. Mother Craig, when asked, in-
> sisted she "would not go a step," even if we did sell and "turn
> her out of doors," as she expressed it. Husband's ardor cooled
> rapidly after that; and while I still longed as ardently as ever
> to go ahead, I could not if he would not! (Memoir, 66)

The difference of opinion between Sarah and Joel here suggests
that Joel had not sufficiently considered the colony scheme's impact on his mother. Sarah's account suggests that he had not
broached the topic with his mother before this, or at least had not
laid out their plans clearly. Since at this point he and Sarah had
been writing letters and making plans for two years, Mrs Craig
must have known something of the scheme, even though she was
often away from home. Whatever the case, it is clear that Sarah's
commitment to the project had not waned, even if Joel's had.

Although they were unable to leave New Brunswick at this
time, they continued their correspondence with the other prospec-

tive colonists in the hope that they would one day be able to join them. In 1866 another of these friends, Preston Maddox, also moved to Kansas.

> He was one of our strong allies; he and family were staunch and zealous followers of the laws of health as then known; his wife and daughter wearing the American costume. They wished to move during summer vacation, the daughter being a teacher. While awaiting belated "marching orders," he had a good offer for his farm; sold it, packed up; *put their goods out on the roadside*: – still no word from us. Then he went for a team to take them to the station, called at the P.O. and found our letter; "and you said Kansas; so to Kansas we are bound as fast at the trains will carry us," he wrote on the cars. They were delighted with S.E. Kansas, and made their home there; as did many other of our fraternity. But we never joined them! (Memoir, 59)

Other families also relocated to Kansas, but the result was not the communal farm, the colony of congenial minds, that Sarah and Joel had longed for. Instead, economic necessity inevitably trumped all other concerns. "Several of our friends went to Kansas; but they nearly always gravitated to where paying work could be had, to await further developments; though some – women as well as men – took up homesteads. But the exact spot for the proposed settlement was never found, and that particular Colony is not located yet" (Memoir, 66).

With their strong ideas and fiery rhetoric, Sarah and Joel might have had the charisma to hold such a group together had they ever been able to start the colony in the first place. On the other hand, their rigid principles and apparent unwillingness to compromise could have proved disastrous in building a community. At any rate, economic obstacles always stood in their way. They were apparently naive enough to believe that, poor as they were, they could launch such a scheme on their own. They were so articulate in print that their correspondents could be forgiven for mistaking them for people of some education and resources. Such was certainly not the case.

Indeed, Sarah describes their "home affairs" as very grim at this time. They tried to farm their land, but the neighbours' cows always managed to trample the crops because "one lame man" (Joel) could not keep the property properly fenced. "So though we farmed all we could each season, we never could raise half a crop. Some falls we housed vegetables, beans and peas enough to last through winter and plant next spring, but often not. In spring how carefully we cut the potatoes to get all the eyes to plant, yet leave a piece for the pot!" (Memoir, 59). Joel managed to get a few odd jobs, which were "a godsend": "Sometimes it was a few rods of road work he would succeed in snatching from the hands of a clique of Irishmen who, as the proverb says, would 'skin a louse for a dollar'; bidding the work down to the lowest notch to get it, in spite of warnings that 'it must be done according to specifications.' When the price ran *too* low, Joel stopped bidding. He often got writing to do, which brought him fair pay – Wills, Deeds, Bonds, and other legal documents; and an occasional job at lumber surveying" (Memoir, 59). As was so often the case, poverty engendered more poverty, in that Joel was often prevented from seizing even the few opportunities suited to his talents: "Years before, he could have been appointed County Lumber Surveyor, if he could have raised the two-and-sixpence, (50c) to 'qualify.' The office was vacant; he, though only about 20, was known to be capable. It was a life office, and one not requiring a tenth of a man's time by the year; but another fellow had the shillings and got the job" (Memoir, 59). In a letter to his mother from this time, Joel assures her that he and his family have not been twenty-four hours without some sort of food, although they had been often hungry. But clearly, a family on the brink of starvation was not one well equipped to embark on a journey to Kansas and build a revolutionary colony. As late as September 1866, Sarah and Joel were still trying to procure lands in Kansas, but with their failure to do so, the colony scheme seemed to collapse.

Sarah's own assessment of the colony project years later in her memoir reveals its true significance in her life: "Though our colony was never settled, and the scheme may be said to have come to naught, it was not without bearing fruit. We gained much useful knowledge; and the intercourse, even by correspondence, with intelligent, progressive minds, was both cheering and helpful; and truly a means of much mental and spiritual uplift – worth tenfold more than it cost us!" (66). These observations offer us a glimpse of the true power of the utopian scheme. Dreaming of creating their own "Eden" gave Sarah and Joel a gleam of hope in the midst of the bleakest poverty, in an isolated life filled with failed business deals, recurrent illness and unemployment, crop failures, and the deaths of beloved children. The dream of a better life in an ideal community made survival in the New Brunswick bush at least somewhat bearable.

Chapter Three

Later Years in New Brunswick

The idealism that drove Sarah and Joel Craig to propose a colony of reformers was channelled, when thwarted, toward other reform causes. In 1867 they became involved in the first temperance society in their district. A movement started by William Rideout of Oak Bay called the Morning Star Temperance Society had gained sudden popularity, and his campaign had resulted in the swift closure of every bar in Eastport, Maine. As soon as a local lodge was organized on the Canadian side of the St Croix River, the Craigs became heavily involved. "One of the first to join the campaign was Dr. James Rouse, then resident at the Rolling Dam ... He espoused the cause with a fierce energy, giving burning lectures and talks on the use of, and traffic in, alcoholics; hurling 'fire and brimstone' right and left on those who 'sell men's souls for gold,' throwing himself into the work with such almost frenzied zeal that ere long, with the aid of Mr Craig and a few others, true as steel – less noisy, but not less ardent – several Divisions were soon organized in the surrounding settlements" (Memoir, 69).

Although Sarah clearly supported the principles of the temperance movement, the enthusiasm expressed in this passage masks a darker subtext. Joel's commitment to the cause was evidently somewhat deeper than hers and his level of involvement much greater than she would have liked. Her views were clearly influenced at least in part by the enlargement of the family and her increased child-care responsibilities. Instead of one baby, Sarah now had three children under the age of four at home, one of whom was an infant. The first local meeting of the Morning Star society took place the evening after the birth of their first daughter, Alice, but Joel was at the meeting anyway, since he was one of the organizers. Sarah's diary entry for 1 July 1867 expresses a surprising level of support and acceptance: "My dear Joel is very kind and gentle towards me, tho' he has to be absent so much. On the evening after my confinement he and William J. attended the organization of the 'Morning Star' Temperance Society at the Rolling Dam, and gave in their names."

However, Joel's involvement in the movement extended far beyond organizational and secretarial duties to donating his time and physical labour toward building the society's new hall. As the months rolled on and he was more and more absent from home, the tone of Sarah's diary entries changes: "J. had to go on Monday, to see to getting the Hall ready to meet in, that evening; and did not return till this afternoon. A thaw came on while he was away; and we were looking anxiously for him to come and get out the potatoes. Sam Parks came here to get some waggon work done, and I got him to dig some. He plowed out about two barrels, near half of which were good, and the rest frozen" (Early diaries, 13 November 1867).

Reading between the lines here, we understand that what Joel had risked by being away was his family's very survival through the winter, since potatoes formed a major part of their diet. Clearly, by the time she wrote about this time in her memoir fifty

years later, Sarah's appraisal of the sacrifices she made for the
Morning Star Society had been sharpened by bitter experience. In
a passage laden with subtext, she barely conceals her frustration at
her husband's excessive involvement in this cause:

> Mr. Craig spent much time during that season working for
> the cause so dear to our hearts; greatly to the detriment of
> our private home interests, which suffered in proportion;
> while he went from place to place with Dr Rouse or alone,
> holding meetings, lecturing, organizing; throwing himself,
> heart, brain and body, yes, and means also (of which we had
> *so little*) into the work. Our Division held its meetings all
> summer in the church; but Dr Rouse urged the building of a
> Hall, which was finally built, on one side of his house – thus
> requiring only *three* walls. Husband *gave* a good bit of lum-
> ber for the new hall; hauling it to the spot, and spending
> many days on it, when he should have been at home. Half
> our crop of potatoes was lost through his absence in good
> weather; and I missed my winter's cloth, by sending my wool
> away just in time to find the carding machine closed for the
> season! (Memoir, 70)

Since producing new clothing for the family depended on this
wool being carded, the implications of Joel's absences were by no
means trivial. Certainly, Sarah supported the temperance work in
whatever way she could; she copied out the society's constitution
and bylaws, wrote a song for the society (Early diaries, 27 October
1867), and attended the meetings whenever possible. But although
she does not say so explicitly, it was probably a great relief to her
when the Morning Star Society split into two warring factions and

then sputtered and died over the winter. "During the winter when men were in the lumber camps, Division meetings were thin; and the glowing promises of great things along literary and social lines in connection with the 'Star' were not being realized. Several Sunday schools were started, and flourished; but the neighborhood libraries, and kindred social and intellectual uplifts never materialized. As often happens, those who might have kept things moving, lacked will and public spirit; the *willing* lacked time, and strength and means. *We* could no longer keep up the pace" (Memoir, 70).

Despite the sense of relief, there is also disappointment here, especially at the promise of intellectual exchange unfulfilled. For Sarah a large part of the value of the temperance movement, like the health-reform crusade, lay in educational opportunities and the formation of a community of congenial minds, rather than simply in the principles of the cause. But that ideal of social exchange and friendship remained elusive. As with their effort to form a colony of reformers, the Craigs were unable to realize their goals because of economic limitations. The talents they had – organizational skills, for instance – were not valued in their rural community and could not put food on the table.

Well-paid work remained largely out of reach because of Joel's disability and the family's isolation. Occasionally, as in August 1868, he would be hired to do some writing, since he could produce a beautiful, clear script. In this case, he was summoned to act as a juror in a medical malpractice suit being tried at the courthouse in St Andrews. Sarah recounts in her diary that her husband ended up not serving as a juror but was "writing for some one; and there being no funds on hand to pay off the jurors he must wait till there is … J. is reporting, or taking notes of, this trial, for

somebody, I am told, who is to pay him for his work, of course."
The trial lasted several weeks, prompting her to lament in her
diary, "I do really long for my dear absent one to return. He never
was away from me so long, since we were married." Unfortunately,
although the trial kept Joel away from home at a critical time in
the farming year, he was *not* paid for his work as promised. Similar bad luck seemed to follow him in other situations; in 1877 a job
cutting railroad ties for an American company that reneged on
the promised wages left Joel and a neighbour in debt, and the
family cow was seized in payment. Much later, in 1881, he was appointed postmaster, and the Craigs had the post office in their
house. This position brought in a bit of steady income, as well as
crowds of neighbours (some of whom were barely literate and
begged Joel or Sarah to write out their letters for them), but it was
not the economic solution they needed.

The constant demands of a large family, and particularly of re-
curring pregnancies, were persistent threats to a woman's health
and happiness. All the water-cure knowledge that Sarah and Joel
possessed could not supply a reliable method of birth control.
Dr Trall had outlined a version of the rhythm method in his book
Sexual Physiology and in articles, but this practice was only par-
tially effective at best. In a painfully honest passage in her diary in
November 1868, Sarah writes:

> But I have made an important discovery – tho' not at first a
> pleasant one – which is that we shall have an addition to our
> family circle, about the last of July next! This is a circum-
> stance I have studied and earnestly endeavoured to avoid,
> being fully convinced that we had children enough for our
> circumstances; and it was my earnest wish to assist my hus-

band in bearing our present burdens rather than laying more on his shoulders at present. He too, has nobly denied himself much of a husband's common privilege, to grant my heart's desire. But we have been outwitted – at least, it is *almost certain* that such is the fact. (Early diaries)

Sarah's hunch was correct, and their fourth son, David James Alexander (Sandy), was born on 26 July 1869. She continued to bear children throughout the next sixteen years, averaging one every two or three years, including another infant that died soon after birth. All the while she was struggling to run a busy house-hold with very scanty means. Her diary entries sometimes reflect her exhaustion. In March 1884, while one of Joel's cousins was staying temporarily at the house, she writes: "March 10th. My health is not good – am feeble and at times can hardly walk about the house: the presence of another person in the house makes the work much heavier. Alice cannot do it all. I am looking forward – not with pleasure, I regret to say – to a family increase, No. 14! To happen about the first of May. This (not being able, nor having proper facilities, to treat myself hygienically) is the cause of my present feebleness."

Despite such challenges, Sarah continued to practise hydropa-thy and was often called out to help nurse members of the com-munity, particularly women who had recently given birth. She reports numerous instances of giving advice on diet and hygiene and occasionally treating severe fevers with water-cure methods. Unfortunately, she could not legally charge a fee for her services without a physician's diploma and could accept only gifts, usually in the form of provisions, in return. She notes wryly that rarely was she rewarded with such gifts for her efforts and was usually sent away empty-handed. Her diary entries suggest a shocking ignorance among the country people as to proper health practices. In a diary entry dated 7 September 1884 she writes: "Mrs J. Montgomery invited us in to dinner. She has a pale, sick girl who has not come to woman's estate nor is likely to unless she has better treatment than her mother or the doctors know how to give. I gave Mrs M. some general directions for hygienic treatment of her daughter and advised her to leave off taking her medicine – a nauseous mixture of iron rust and other dirty trash. But I have not much faith in her recovery where there is so much ignorance and so much of killing fashions." Fortunately, a few weeks later, on 21 September, Sarah notes of this case, "The girl I prescribed for two weeks ago, was well enough to go to meeting today – said she had quit taking her medicine. She *may* recover – *would* if she throws away her corsets, keeps her hands and feet warm, her head cool, and gets her pores open."

In another case Sarah was called out to treat an ailing infant:

The little one appeared death-struck, when I first saw him but I was puzzled as to the disease; I could not name it. At last I took opportunity to question the father closely as to its previous treatment; he tho't this had been very simple but my suspicions were aroused and I asked if they had bathed it with alcohol. He confessed they had, and I finally learned that it had had *alcohol and wormwood* applied to its bowels! And it under three weeks old! I spoke strongly of the danger of such treatment; but the father pled ignorance of the laws of health. I told him I would send him some *books* in hygiene if he would study them, which he agreed to do. The little one brightened up after awhile; and for sake of its anxious parents I hope it *may* get well, but it looks very doubtful. He

paid me 50 cents and Andrew bro't me home. (Early diaries,
4 December 1886)

Unfortunately, the advice came too late, and a few days later the
baby died. Despite such setbacks, Sarah could not bring herself to
refuse help to her sick neighbours. She wrote in her memoir that
"such service – ministering to the sick – was my great delight; but
did not make me rich in worldly goods" (97).

Water-cure methods did not always work, however, even when
carefully followed according to the "highest up to date authority
in Hygieotherapy" (Memoir, 83), as the tragic loss of two of the
Craig children to scarlet fever in 1874 makes only too clear. Apparently, there was a "world pandemic" of scarlet fever (also called
scarlatina) between 1820 and 1880, in both Europe and North
America.[1] Scarlet fever is caused by group A streptococcus (the
same bacterium that causes strep throat) and is now easily treated
with antibiotics. But in the nineteenth century, before antibiotics
were available, the disease could be very serious indeed, causing
not only an itchy rash and high fever but also "inflammation of
lymph nodes and abscessing of the throat and tonsils."[2] It could
also lead to complications such as rheumatic fever and meningi-
tis and long-term effects such as heart, liver, and kidney damage.[3]
Young children between the ages of two and eight were at particularly high risk; infants seemed to derive some resistance from
their mother's milk and were thus more likely to survive than their
toddler siblings.[4] Many children died of scarlet fever during this
prolonged pandemic. Those suffering from poor nutrition were
particularly vulnerable.[5]

Sarah writes in her memoir that she had seen only a couple of
mild cases of scarlet fever before, and so felt she had little to fear from
the disease when it started making the rounds of her community.

Indeed, the account of her water-cure treatments published in the August 1864 volume of the *Herald of Health* includes a description of how she treated her own ten-year-old brother Edwin for scarlet fever. She notes that she followed the treatment laid out in "Dr Charles Munde's 'Hydriatic Treatment of Scarlet Fever,'" a book published in 1857 that described various types of scarlatina and their hydropathic treatment with wet-sheet packs.[6] In her published report, Sarah claims that Edwin recovered in ten days.[7] Her confidence in treating this disease may also have been boosted by accounts of scarlet fever treatment through hygieotherapy such as that published in the *Water-Cure Journal* in June 1858. Thus she believed that she had little to fear. This conviction led to tragic consequences: she tells of how she inadvertently brought the sickness home to her own family.

> Mrs McDermot's daughter Nancy was then living, a widow with two children, in her mother's house. Her children took the disease; the baby died of it – and the drug treatment. With heart full of sisterly sympathy for my dear friend, I went to condole with her. It was a most rash, foolhardy act; but I believed myself so fully armed by faith as to be invulnerable – proof against the Devil's artillery! Too late I realized that I had been actuated rather by a spirit of bravado than faith; – rather with a feeling of going where others were afraid to go – than in humble trust in the power of the Great Physician. (Memoir, 82)

Sarah visited the McDermots several more times, and eventually all the Craig children caught it. Several of these cases were mild, but others were severe. Unfortunately, Charles Munde, whose book *Hydriatic Treatment of Scarlet Fever* she consulted, claimed that adults were more at risk than children, whereas this is not the case; his views may have misled Sarah and Joel into believing that the younger children were not vulnerable. Yet with the youngest, Joel Bonney, still an infant, and the father, Joel himself, never strong, the whole family was soon laid low in various ways:

> Now came the "tug of war." Albert, Frank and baby Joel B. had the rash lightly, required little nursing comparatively, and when the rash went off, got well readily. With the other three, when the rash and fever turned, the nostrils and ears began to run poisonous, fetid matter; the throats inflamed, swelling in lumps under the ears, requiring to be kept constantly cool with wet cloths, and sometimes snow or ice. In fact, they really needed such unremitting care, day and night, that too often *something* would be overlooked – the cold compresses, perhaps. There were but our two selves to stand to it all; and several nights the father was too sick himself to sit up. During those weeks, I did my washing and scrubbing mostly in the night, *to keep myself awake!* (Early diaries, March 1874)

Alice lost most of her hair and was weak for many weeks, but she eventually recovered. Whether her health problems later on in her twenties could be traced back to this bout of scarlet fever is anyone's guess, but considering the potential long-term effects that the disease could have (damage to the heart, liver, or kidneys, for example), it is possible. However, two of the youngest Craig children died, despite Joel and Sarah's application of all the water-cure methods they knew. Three-year-old Clara Matilda was extremely ill:

The tenth day she began to pass blood from the bowels, and nearly bled to death. But a vigorous application of *cold* water by injection and cold wet cloths on the abdomen, conquered this symptom. After some days the bowels resumed natural action, tho the child persistently refused all nourishment but milk. She had lost her voice for a few days but regained it; and when I spoke to her about getting well, she said "No"... I asked "Are you going to die and leave papa and me?" "Yes!" she replied, confidently. Dear little "Brown-top"! How keenly I remembered these words, after she had been laid away on the hill. She had looked into a world where there is no sickness, and knew she was going there to stay. (Memoir, 83)

Four-year-old Sandy became deaf from the disease and was the first child to succumb:

March 31st, about three o'clock in the morning, when I took my place as watcher, we both knew the end was not far off. Husband told me how Sandy had been calling and pleading for papa to help him! "I *can't* climb over this big log!" he mourned; "please help me!" His voice had a strange note in it after he grew deaf –like one speaking in a room alone, and listening for a sign of being heard. About 5 o'clock I roused his papa, and we stood by our dear, noble boy, while he met and wrestled with the grim monster, and *were unable to help him!* (Early diaries, 1874)

Little Clara died only a few hours after her brother, and sorrowfully Sarah and Joel "laid the little bodies away on the hill ... and

returned to our half-desolated home, and the care of those mer-
cifully left to us" (Early diaries, 1874). Two weeks of constant
cleaning and washing ensued, with the help of both Sarah's and
Joel's mothers, but once the grandmothers had departed, depression set in: "Oh, then! In the unwonted stillness of the home, the
wave of loneliness that came sweeping over me for the bright ones
gone from our arms, not the sweet patience of gentle Alice, the
suddenly active boyish spirits of the older boys, could dispel."

Sarah's diary account of this episode is written as a "Retro-
spective" covering the years between 1871 and 1879, and when she
includes this narrative, somewhat expanded, in her memoir, it is
clear that her grief is still fresh even after the passage of more than
four decades. In her memoir she pays tribute to these little lost
ones. First, she remembers "Sandy the quick, the energetic, ever
alert, irrepressible; as his papa described him once to a friend, the
'wide-awake go everywhere'... the brightest, most promising of
our flock. Life to him was a pure delight!" (84). She then recalls
Clara: "And what can I write of my 'wee fairie maiden'? or how tell
of her sweet endearing ways that were like daily manna to my
mother heart? And how I thank our Father that, though she so
soon was removed from our sight – 'not lost, but gone before,' – I
had the sweet privilege of being her mother, and enjoying her love-
liness even those few years! Like her brother Sandy, she was
thoughtful and wise beyond her years; but her capacity for *loving*
was her chief charm" (Memoir, 85).

It is worth noting that Sarah and Joel in no way saw their
inability to save their children as a failure of the water-cure system itself, but instead attributed it in part to their inadequate
resources for medical treatment: "With these two, it had been a

hand to hand struggle with death from the first; and had our *faith*
and our *facilities for treating disease* been equal to our knowledge
of Hygeiotherapy, we *might*, with God's help, have saved them"
(Early diaries, 1874). Sarah was clearly aware that their backwoods
cabin was not the cleanest environment for effective doctoring.
Thus, in spite of this serious setback and what it suggested about
the limitations of the water-cure method, she continued to use it
for years to come.

Although the years blunted the sorrow of losing these little
ones, they were never forgotten. In her memoir Sarah mentions
visiting their graves in 1881 during a "flying visit" from her brother
Henry and his wife: "In the afternoon we all took a walk to the
North-east hill-top overlooking the lake. Here is our little 'ceme-
tery' and from here is a fine, panoramic view of lake and forest,
mountain, hill and valley" (Memoir, 97–8). Her love of panoramic
views, often expressed in her diary and memoir, must always have
been associated with this small collection of graves.

Sarah persisted in wearing her reform dress, and it continued
to cause occasional friction in both family and community. Her
sister Martha's abrupt abandonment of the reform costume provoked a crisis in Sarah's relations with her family. It appears that
during the summer of 1867 Martha made herself a long dress (with
hoops) and wore it to town while family members helped her to
keep the matter secret from Sarah, whose reaction they predicted
only too well. This episode occurred during the first flowering of
the Morning Star Temperance Society, and Martha had been wearing her long dress for more than two months before Sarah found
out. Sarah mentions the incident only briefly in her memoir, with
the comment that her readers (her children) would not understand her attitude, but her diary entries are filled with anguish.

Her extreme reaction indicates how important the dress-reform issue was to her. Her diary entry for 16 September 1867 reads: "Mother was here last week and told me the tale, which has almost overwhelmed me (and my husband too,) with grief and shame! I feel as if I had almost lost my sister! We have stood together so many years, and hand in hand stemmed the tide of public opinion, till it has more than begun to ebb, how can she, in the face of repeated, and most solemn pledges, turn her back upon her principles, and betray the confidence of her dearest friends, in such a way? I can hardly realize it."

Martha claimed that she had been drawn into wearing the American Costume while she was still too young to make such a decision herself. Regardless of the reasons, to Sarah and Joel her actions amounted to "backsliding" (Memoir, 72) and called for urgent prayers on Martha's behalf. It did not seem to matter that their temperance society was filled with women members who were Christians but not dress reformers. Martha's attendance at the meetings in a long dress seemed to provoke more disapproval than she would have if she had not attended at all. Sarah's diary entry for 1 October 1867 reflects this attitude: "Yesterday was a cold, blowy day; and I could not go to the meeting. But my sister was there *in her robes of dishonor.* She and 15 others signed the Pledge. We must still hope and pray for her; and win her back by love, with the help of our Saviour!"

Sarah's extension of religious language and principles to the cause of dress reform is not unique among reformers of the era. As noted earlier, the leaders of the water-cure movement had always linked the cause of health reform with Christianity. They especially liked to repeat St Paul's admonition to the Romans to "present your bodies a living sacrifice, holy and acceptable unto

God" (Romans 12:1). Indeed, this passage was quoted by James Jackson in his address at the opening of his water-cure establishment in Dansville, New York, and reprinted in the *Water-Cure Journal* for December 1858. However, exactly what constituted the correct presentation of the body (especially a woman's body) to God was the subject of much debate among Christians. Sarah implicitly acknowledges this controversy in a remark in her handwritten memoir (not included by Florence in the typescript), when she concludes her account of this episode by saying, "Of how this 'backsliding' of our beloved sister affected us I will say little here; my readers would neither understand nor appreciate our attitude." Although Sarah and Martha eventually reconciled, this was clearly a painful period for both of them.

Sarah's insistence on wearing her reform dress also caused her to deliberately isolate herself from her spiritual community. In the absence of close ties with her church, her diary entries for 1868 are filled with longing for a closer relationship with God. She even sought spiritual guidance from John Humphrey Noyes, the charismatic founder and leader of the Oneida Community, one of the very few successful nineteenth-century utopian colonies, who was also a theologian of sorts and the author of numerous religious tracts. She may also have been aware that the Oneida Community believed women and men to be equals and that the Oneida women all wore a version of the reform dress. She was clearly aware of Noyes's main teachings: that Christ's second coming had already taken place (in 70 CE), but in a spiritual sense; "a second and final resurrection and judgment was now approaching."[8] He proclaimed that he and his devoted followers could bring about the kingdom of God on earth by separating themselves from sin and living in "perfection"; this belief assumed, not a final state of the soul that could not be improved upon, but rather "an inner sense of assurance of salvation from sin."[9]

Sarah may have felt comfortable writing to Noyes for spiritual advice knowing that his community adhered to many of her own beliefs about social reform. "Jan. 27th, 1868. I have had a feeling lately, that I *must* write to Mr John H. Noyes, for light. I believe him to be a holy, and inspired man, capable of leading me in the path of holiness. He is the Veteran of Perfectionism, the discoverer, I believe of the fact that Christ's Second Coming is a past event. What human, better fitted than he, to feed 'babes in Christ?'" (Early diaries). Sarah may not have realized that the Oneida Community practised "complex marriage," a type of partnering that eschewed exclusive marital pairing and taught instead that "each should be married to all" in the community.[10] Neither she nor Joel would have approved of such a system of multiple heterosexual relationships, which some labelled "free love." She makes no mention of a response from Noyes to her letter, but her desperate attempts to reach out to others who shared her spiritual concerns suggests a questing spirit and a deep loneliness.

Sarah records how, several years later, she came to be baptized at last, after the minister came to their home to talk to her about the possibility:

May 30, 1871 … I replied, that I had never felt ready yet; stated that I had been secluded entirely from meeting for a number of years, partly on account of my peculiar style of dress – not wishing to provoke unnecessary remark, or divert people's minds from the one object they should have in view when attending divine worship. And feeling that I should be dishonoring my Master by conforming to the foolish fashions of this world, I had always preferred to remain at home, and read, sing, or write, and learn of the Master's will ... from the bible.

"Well," said he, "God is everywhere; talk to the Master about it, I can wait upon you almost any time; whenever you feel ready to follow the Savior, in His appointed way." (Early diaries)

Very soon after this visit, Sarah was indeed baptized, and diary entries from the 1880s indicate that she often attended church then. But the conflicted impulses expressed in this passage – longing to be part of the church community and at the same time tenaciously clinging to her principles on dress – are clear. By this point, they had obviously caused her years of acute loneliness.

This deep sense of isolation may be in part responsible for her extraordinary lapse in judgment while she was visiting her parents in St Stephen in August 1883:

August 12th Sunday. Sister Lottie [her brother Edwin's wife] is sick or at least ill with a complication of troubles – under the doctor's hands but out of danger, we trust. Mrs Nary Senior has been staying with her, helping mother in the care of the children, and the house-work. She went with me down town to sell my berries. While I was preparing, she came up, embraced and kissed me, and "wished I would let her coax me." "What way?" I asked, not in the least guessing her meaning. "To put on a long dress." Taken quite by surprise – not having my armor tightly girded on (as I have had little or no fighting to do for some years), reasons, arguments, pledges, formerly ever ready, [and] now almost I might say for the time, quite forgotten – I allowed her to persuade me to put on one of mother's dresses to go shopping in. I got on very smoothly; but felt guilty and ashamed in the presence of those who know my face and Reform Dress too. And I would not again run the risks of falls, and severe injuries, that I ran during those few hours for a good deal, to say the least.

But I did not begin to realize how deeply I had sinned in violating conscience and principle, and trampling on my husband's and my own convictions of right and truth, until after I came home and told J. how I had been "betrayed by a kiss." For some hours he seemed almost beside himself with anguish and could not bear that I should touch him as if my touch was pollution! But I will not try to pen the experience of those hours: I will only say that we have both been deeply tho' not fatally wounded; and I at least will be more watchful in future and try to keep my armor brighter. (Early diaries)

This startling account suggests that Joel was as much an influence on Sarah in her tenacious adherence to the reform dress as were her own principles or those of the reform movement at large. His reaction seems so extreme that we might wonder if she would have been more likely to compromise earlier if he had not lived as long as he did. It also raises troubling questions about her actual freedom of choice in the matter: having defied the patriarchal system (or so she thought) by refusing to wear the restrictive female garb dictated by fashion, was she at the same time imprisoned in that choice by her desire to please a husband who held such rigid and uncompromising views? It is impossible to tell, but this experience of failure and shame surely influenced her reactions to the similar predicament of her daughter Alice a few years later.

A passionate *cri du cœur* scribbled on a scrap of paper sometime in the 1880s suggests that Sarah's longing for broader social horizons for herself and their children had become at times a point of contention between herself and Joel. Her husband, nearly worn out by hard work and bad luck, had apparently lost most of his earlier fervour for moving away to seek greener pastures. Clearly referring to the original colony scheme, she writes:

> I wished to go, to help make a home where we could live by our labor without being *slaves*; where our children could have privileges – social, intellectual, moral privileges they never could enjoy here. I had many reasons for wishing to go to a new country. These wishes were born when my husband shared my wishes and plans; in fact *he was the father of the plan and the wish*, and thought the reasons *good – I* think so still. The wish, in its fulness, became *a part of my life* thenceforth; it has been *crushed, smothered*, held down, ignored, perhaps *he* thought it *dead*. But a little air and sunshine have started it to a new life, as vigorous as ever. And O, I feel as if this pent up longing of a score of years must at last be recognized. Several of our children have grown up, others half way up, among the "rabble of ignorant gossipping scandalmongers of Whittier's Ridge": perhaps their father is willing the rest of the family should grow up here, without any *systematic* schooling, lest they should learn more evil than good. *I am not!*

Sarah's frustration is evident in this harsh condemnation of her community. Although she and her family were never "slaves," her use of the word here expresses her rage at her family's persistent poverty. More broadly, she also longed for the types of "social, intellectual, moral privileges" for her children which her New Brunswick community had never been able to provide.

This heartfelt cry was likely written in the mid-1880s during a revival of interest in forming a utopian community prompted by two of her oldest children. Some details of this new scheme are revealed in both Sarah's diaries and in the exceedingly brief (eighteen-month) diary kept by the Craigs' eldest daughter, Alice. It seems that Frank had come back from a stint working in St Stephen fired up with the idea of reviving the colony scheme. He and Alice spent considerable time writing up some sort of manifesto for this proposed colony: "May 10th 1885. Sunday. This has been a busy week. Frank and I have prepared, during odd minutes, a statement of our Colony plan, and with Alice's help, copied it out, and sent it to several papers both in Canada and the United States, under the head 'A Call for Volunteers.' Prayers have been sent with and after them; and may God, our loving Father, prosper the mission of those little sheets, and grant us at last the fulfilment of our hopes!" (Early diaries).

Joel was apparently much less enthusiastic than his wife and children, but he was content to wait and see if the plan took hold. Any possible connection was revived, and every former contact written to; in June Sarah records: "June 23, 1885. I wrote to brother Isaac, to learn if he could give us the addresses of any of our old 'Colony' correspondents, or any word of their present whereabouts. I also wrote two double cards to the 'Witness' and the

'Visitor' to learn if our 'Call for Volunteers' had been received. So we sent a big mail tonight" (Early diaries).

Clearly, Sarah had other plans in mind as well. On 30 June she records that she wrote a letter to "Harriet N. Austin, MD Dansville, NY." This of course was the famous dress reformer and water-cure practitioner who was one of the key physicians at Our Home on the Hillside. She was also perhaps Sarah's strongest role model, being an educated woman who had qualified as a hydropathic physician and had regularly written eloquent articles for the *Water-Cure Journal* and the *Herald of Health* for years. By 19 July there was still no response to the "Call for Volunteers," but 21 July brought "a loving letter from Miss Dr Austin, accompanied by some numbers of the 'Laws of Life,' and some tracts and lectures on the Gospel of Health in connection with the Gospel of Grace. How cheering! How delightful, thus to clasp hands and renew our acquaintance with these dear friends (Drs Jackson and Austin), noble apostles of the Health reform!" (Early diaries, 21 July 1885).

Despite such moral support from powerful allies, the practical details of settling a colony in the west continued to elude the family. In August Sarah received a letter from her brother Henry, to whom she had also written inquiring about possibilities, and his news was not encouraging: "I wrote to him, some time ago, asking some questions of a man who works with him and owns some 1800 sheep *in Kansas*, concerning the natural advantages, climate &c of the country. Henry wrote me a *very* discouraging letter on this man's authority, with a rather absurd and ridiculous story of pioneers' hardships – not in Kansas but in Nebraska; and winds up by advising us not to 'jump out of the frying pan into the fire'" (Early diaries, 4 August 1885). The news from Sarah's older brother,

Isaac, the other idealist of the Jameson family, who had moved west with his wife and children years before, was likewise discouraging. By the 1880s Isaac had joined and then quit a "humbug" community (a utopian colony of some sort) in Missouri; he had left it disillusioned and was now having a very hard time supporting his wife and four children.

There was, however, another possibility: that, with the support of Harriet Austin, Alice and perhaps even Frank might gain employment at Our Home on the Hillside in Dansville, the famous centre for water-cure therapy. This scheme is revealed in a number of entries in Sarah's diary for 1884–86 and in the diary briefly kept by Alice herself. In an entry dated 20 January 1884, Sarah notes, "I wrote to Brother William, requesting him to consider a proposition for assisting Alice to gain a medical education." This may have been a request for financial support in helping Alice to travel to Dansville, where she might be able to get training, starting out in the position of "bath girl." It seems that Alice too was writing to other members of her mother's family. In her entry for 22 March 1885, she notes that she wrote to "Aunt Ella," who was the wife of Sarah's brother Henry: "22nd ... today I thought I want to write and tell her that I have the promise of a situation at 'Our Home,' and that I have some prospect of going there this Spring. It will take some money, of course, and I don't know where it is coming from, but mother says she thinks she does. If it don't come this Spring I can wait. I am sure of a chance there now, whenever I can go" (Diary of Martha Alice Craig).

Alice may have inquired about financial support from Ella and Henry, although she does not mention this specifically in her diary entry. Henry was the brother from whom Sarah would receive the disappointing letter in August. Other family members, however, were more encouraging; on 3 April 1885, Sarah writes: "Received a letter from Brother William, in which he confirmed the offer of money to pay Alice's way to Dansville. Her father is not favorable to the plan. But we will wait and pray." William had long been a supporter of the water-cure system, and was one of the more successful members of the Jameson clan, having been employed by the William Rogers Silver works for some years. His financial support would be crucial to such a scheme. Alice also kept up a lively correspondence that year with her cousin Flora, the daughter of Sarah's brother Isaac, who was in rather dire straits at the time; the family ended up living in a tent for part of that year.

An entry in Alice's diary gives further insight into the debate on this issue between her parents:

June 26th My birthday. I am 18 years old today. I have about given up the idea of going to Dansville this year. If I cannot go this year I can wait. There is plenty to do at home. But I mean to go some time, if I live long enough. Not that I am afraid I will not get a chance, for I am pretty sure of that; but Father does not like the idea at all and thinks I had better stay at home for a while, until I know enough about house-keeping to make a smart, capable, and economical *wife* for somebody! *Somebody's wife!* Well, "Somebody" keeps himself strangely from view, and I hope he will for a few years, at any rate, untill I have a good education, and can support my self. (Diary of Martha Alice Craig, 1885)

Joel's objections to his daughter's aspirations seem odd, considering his views on women's equality. But it is certainly clear from Sarah's remarks throughout her diaries that Alice was indispensable to her in helping with the household work; when Alice was away, the housekeeping always got seriously behind. As Sarah writes when a prolonged visit to Martha's is proposed, "But how can I spare her with all this family to work for? There is more work here, right *in the house* than both of us have ever been able to keep up with. I get on with the house work pretty well, but get little time to sew, and the sewing is running behind. The washing and scrubbing are quite too hard for me to do alone, Lucy is not strong enough to do much yet either, and can only help at the cooking" (Early diaries, 30 March 1886). In a rural household, keeping the floors clean (by sweeping and scrubbing), especially in a house with young children, must have been a constant laborious task and one that required a good deal of strength and endurance. The need for Alice's help may have been at the bottom of Joel's reluctance to let her leave. He was likely also aware that, without financial aid, they could never afford to send either Alice or Frank as far away as New York.

Indeed, during these years every member of the family had to contribute to keeping food on the table. Frank worked away part of the time, in Connecticut and Maine, doing anything that came along: peeling bark, haying, delivering milk for a dairy, or selling rubber stamps and window locks door to door on commission. In November 1885 Albert, Frank, and their father worked together bottling and selling several homemade remedies called "Magic Tooth-ache Killer," "Pain Expeller," and "Craig's Peerless Plaster," which Frank sold along with his window and door locks. Sarah herself spent part of 1885 tramping from one house to another trying to sell a decorative "Family Record" on commission. Each of these efforts yielded some income, but it was never enough.

Albert was also working away part of the time, doing manual labour in the woods and trying to earn enough to send some money home to the family.

Entries in Sarah's diaries for 1885 and 1886 suggest, however, that there were tensions between him and the family. In summarizing a letter received from Albert in March 1885, she relates that he had not written home for months because he could not send any money along with the letters; he felt that "the fates or the furies seem[ed] to have combined against him," and he was very bitter. She goes on to say, "Don't think he will come home before fall, as he wants to come home a little better off, is sick of coming home to be told he had not done anything &c. Poor boy! I don't know whether he refers to the neighbors in that sentence, or to some unfortunate unkindly remark made at home. I am sorry to say that the happiest relations did not always exist between him and the rest of the family when he was at home. But we love him very much, notwithstanding his sometimes unlovely temper" (Early diaries, 10 March 1885). This is the first mention she makes anywhere of Albert's "unlovely temper," but we catch a glimpse here of the psychological and emotional toll that the family's desperate poverty had taken on the children. It must have been very frustrating for the eldest son to see that an escape from such poverty remained just out of his reach, and that although he could earn enough to cover his own expenses (barely), he could seldom make enough to help the rest of his family.

With the pressing financial needs of the family in mind, Sarah persevered in her quest to make the connections necessary for Alice to go to Dansville:

14th April 1885. I sent a letter to E.D. Leffingwell "Our Home,"

Dansville NY to enquire if there was a place waiting for Alice, and I also bespoke a chance for Frank, stating a few of the things he could turn his hand to. I also ordered a copy of the Herald of Health.

Sept. 22nd. I received a note from Mrs E. Fowler Wells, publisher of Phrenological Journal, in answer to some inquiries respecting a colony in Kansas to which Mr Wells (deceased) was Secretary. She could not tell me much about them, but gave their address. (Early diaries)

Unfortunately, there is no evidence that such inquiries bore fruit in the form of positions for Alice and Frank.

In 1886 the issue of dress was causing a tug-of-war between Sarah and her sister, Martha. After abandoning the short dress and trousers herself years earlier, Martha sought to encourage the eighteen-year-old Alice to do the same during Alice's visits to St Stephen, where Martha lived. Interestingly, this incident is recorded in both Sarah's and Alice's diaries. On 30 March 1886 Sarah comments:

[Alice] writes me all about her visit, and how she enjoys it, of her aunt's plans for her, which she don't think well suit me; and says "Aunt made, without my knowledge, a skirt 2 or 3 inches longer than my stuff dress for me to go out in." I knew Martha would use her influence that way, but did not think she would go so far. Alice's dress is several inches longer than the true reform dress; is within nine inches of the floor – as much of a compromise to public opinion as we can afford. But Martha cannot bear to be seen with a woman who has a suspicion of pants to be seen about her. So Alice not wishing to oppose her aunt and wishing to go to the meetings yielded *under protest*. But she assures me she will always be a dress reformer, and I believe she will. (Early diaries)

Sarah's account here is very restrained, but her hopes for Alice's continued adherence to the dress-reform cause is hinted at numerous times in her diaries. For example, in October 1884 she describes a "very pretty" pencil drawing that Alice had made to send to her cousin Flora, with whom she frequently corresponded, as a birthday gift. Sarah describes Alice's drawing as depicting a girl dressed in a short dress and trousers holding a bunch of flowers, and she notes that "she made a copy of her picture today for her father. I named it 'The Girl of the Future.' She called the first one 'A Young Hygienist'" (Early diaries, 26 October 1884). Sarah's title for the drawing seems freighted with her own hopes for Alice's future, one that she might share with other young women in a more enlightened age. And by giving this title to the copy that Alice made for Joel, Sarah also affirms to her husband her vision of their daughter's future.

Alice's own account of the incident with Aunt Martha comes at the end of several entries describing her extended visit with her aunt and cousins in St Stephen, and how much she has been enjoying herself. Notably, her entries lack the fervent language that so marks her mother's writing on this subject. "Aunt Martha had made up her mind that I was going to stay three or four weeks at least, and has been trying to persuade mother to let me stay and learn the Tailoress trade, but I knew she could not spare me, just now, at any rate. She made me a long skirt to wear on the street – not very long, but still long enough to be inconvenient. I didn't like to wear it, but I wanted to go to the Temperance Lecture, and as she wouldn't take me in my short dress, I did wear it there, and to the other meetings I attended" (Diary of Martha Alice Craig, 1 April 1886).

Neither Sarah's nor Alice's account mentions Alice having to wear a corset as well, and Martha undoubtedly knew that requiring Alice to put on such a garment would be going too far. Although hoops had by this time gone out of fashion, corsets had not, and the heaviness of conventional dresses, combined with the pressures placed on the female internal organs from the tight-lacing of corsets, continued to pose a serious threat to female health. Medical practitioners, both conventional allopathic doctors and water-cure physicians, still warned of the dangers of tight-lacing to women's health and especially to women of child-bearing age. Even if health problems were not immediately apparent, the physical effects of wearing corsets were dramatic: Mary E. Tillotson wrote that when she abandoned her corsets, her waist measured only nineteen inches, but it slowly expanded as she recovered her health.[11] It seems unlikely that Alice would have agreed to wear a corset of any kind.

Sarah's summary of a letter she received from Martha after Alice's March visit is full of her usual fiery zeal on the dress-reform issue:

Martha wrote to me too, and says among other things, "You brought Alice up your way, now why not let her choose for herself?" Dear, kind, loving *weak* sister! Alice *did* choose for herself years ago – chose as her mother did to be a pioneer in the cause of Woman's emancipation from fashion. She knows too well the truth and principles which underlie my choice and the cause, to choose otherwise. Are not women sicken-

ing, suffering and dying all around us for want of some one
to show them in its true light, the hideous deformity of the
cruel tyrant Fashion? (Early diaries, 21 April 1886)

Sarah's stand on the issue received encouragement from other
female reformers. Their cause had been bolstered in the 1880s by
the formation of the National Council of Women, dedicated to
women's suffrage, which also mandated the formation of a "dress
committee" to study women's clothing and what changes could
be made that would be acceptable to the broad population of
women.[12] Shortly after Alice returned home from St Stephen,
Sarah received welcome news in this matter: "April 21st 1886. I received a noble letter from Mrs E.B. Harman [Ellen Beard Harman, one of the hydropathic physicians who had graduated from
Trall's Hygeio-Therapeutic College], whom I used to know as a
most uncompromising dress-reformer; her letter is so full of sym-
pathy and encouragement for the present, strength and faith in
the cause and in the future, that Alice feels inspired to take a more
decided stand than ever" (Early diaries).

Martha's forceful insistence that Alice wear a long skirt in town
may have signalled more than just her own prejudices. Certainly,
she was able to see how wearing the reform dress was hindering
her niece's ability to make her way as an adult woman in the
world. Sarah remained isolated in her country home much of the
time, travelling to town only rarely. But at eighteen Alice clearly
wanted more social contact. Even her acceptance at rural temperance meetings was undermined by her style of dress, as Sarah
admits in a diary entry for 31 August 1886: "A division of 'Sons of
Temperance' has been organized at the Rolling Dam lately; Frank

joined the first meeting. Alice sent in her name last week and went over tonight, to join; but was blackballed on account of her dress!" From her time spent in St Stephen with her aunt enjoying the benefits of town life, Alice herself must have understood that wearing the reform dress cut her off from the few economic and social opportunities available to a young woman of scanty means in late nineteenth-century rural New Brunswick. If Sarah had any appreciation of the obstacles facing her daughter, she does not hint at it in her diaries. However, her continuing efforts to forge links with Our Home on the Hillside and secure a job there for Alice suggests her awareness of opportunities elsewhere. Considering the amount of household work Alice did at home, Sarah's willingness to let her daughter go to New York for the sake of a brighter future is commendable, even if her plans ultimately failed to materialize.

In fact, Martha's interest in having Alice stay with her in St Stephen was not completely altruistic: she too needed a girl to help her at home. Recently widowed, she was earning a living at the one occupation that was available to her: doing housework for others. As Alice notes in her diary for 14 April 1886, Martha was extremely busy during spring-cleaning time that year, "cleaning house for nearly all the town." Her sons, Emery and Stanley, were working at a store to supplement the family income, but boys could not be expected to scrub floors, wash dishes, and do laundry. Martha needed a girl like Alice to keep her house in order while she was cleaning everyone else's and exhausting herself in the process. Alice notes a couple of times in her diary that Martha stayed home from work because she was not feeling well. In June, while Alice was staying with her again, Sarah reports, "She will have to stay a while, as her aunt has worked herself sick and is resting, under the doctor's orders not to go out house cleaning any more."

Although Sarah does not mention the issue in her diaries, the conflict with her sister over Alice's future as a dress reformer played out against the backdrop of a split in the ranks of crusaders for women's rights. Some of the most prominent of these, such as Amelia Bloomer, Susan B. Anthony, and Elizabeth Cady Stanton, had long since come to see dress reform and the hostility it generated as a distraction from the real issues: votes for women, legal equality, and a reform of social and institutional beliefs that perpetuated notions of women's weakness.[13] Anthony is said to have complained that at one lecture "the attention of my audience was fixed upon my clothes instead of my words."[14] But women on the other side of the issue had their own objections: in 1885 Mary E. Tillotson charged that dress reformers were "treated as an embarrassment at women's rights events."[15] However, since the reformers often used an evangelical tone in their attacks on those who had abandoned the short dress and trousers, this response is perhaps not surprising. Whether or not Martha knew anything about this split in the forces of feminism, she understood that Alice's future prosperity could not lie within the marginalized and dwindling community of dress reformers.

Her scheme to get Alice some training in the tailoring trade actually bore fruit for a time. In October 1886 Sarah noted in her diary that her daughter was going to St Stephen to take her place in a newly opened tailor's shop. Alice even had an apprentice working under her for a short time in 1887: "Alice went to work in the shop on Monday and is stitching away trying to earn money to replenish our flour barrel, which has been empty for some time ... Alice will have an apprentice next week; she has written to

Almeda McRae to go over at once. Medie [Almeda] spoke to Alice
to get her a chance to learn the trade if she could, and the chance
was there all right. This will help Alice's wages, as she is working
by the piece, and will get paid, for all she and her apprentice can
make" (Early diaries, 7 April 1887). In light of this success, it is odd
that Alice seems not to have continued her tailoring work when
the family later moved to New Jersey. Perhaps her adherence to
the reform dress (if she continued to wear the outfit) marked her
as too eccentric to be employed in a business that in most places
required constant interaction with the public. Or perhaps her
training in St Stephen had simply not been extensive enough to
prepare her for what were undoubtedly the more sophisticated
towns of New Jersey. Whatever the reason, she seems never to have
held such employment again after the family left New Brunswick.
Instead, she spent years doing the kind of heavy housework that
would eventually kill her.

Late in 1885 Joel had become a licensed preacher and started
travelling out to remote communities (usually on foot) to preach.
Although Sarah notes in her diary that his heart had been set on
doing this work for years, it is astonishing that a man who had
suffered frail health for most of his life should embark on such an
enterprise, one that seems to have paid very little. The fact that he
set out on his first "missionary tour" on 31 December 1885 is similarly surprising, although the frozen roads would have made travel
easier. However, it is clear that walking long distances in freezing
weather did nothing to improve his health; he was laid low for several weeks in February, and on 9 March Sarah wrote that, although
he had been able to go to Rolling Dam and back, "his health is
very frail – a very little fatigues him." Although he recovered somewhat after this episode, Sarah notes on 19 May that his ill health

was having a serious impact on the family's farming activities: "We are just beginning to plant our garden. Joel is *very weak*, when he takes hold of the plough, and the old mare is not much better." A further note at the beginning of June indicates that he was much the same, being able to plow only a few furrows at a time for the children to sow seeds in; he then had to lie down to rest for a while before rising to plow any more. No diagnosis of his condition is mentioned (indeed, without modern medical equipment, perhaps none was possible), but he seems to have improved enough over the summer to walk regularly to church and back with the older children.

On 17 September, however, Joel suffered a stroke. He had apparently been trying to renew the old dam above the lake to build a workshop where he could set up his "turning lathe and jig-saw" and teach the younger boys to use them and the other tools. He had been doing some strenuous work; he and Frank and another boy were laying timbers when he fell. Fortunately, the others were able to help him to stumble back home. He lay dying for almost three weeks, and although he had been gravely ill many times before and had always recovered, Sarah gradually realized that this time he would not. Her diary entries eloquently express her anguish:

Oct. 1, 1886. Today my heart grew very sore at the tho't of his leaving me and the children just now, and all his unfinished work – physical, mental and spiritual; and especially, thinking of how he has bro't on his sickness and probable death by unseasonable and unreasonable efforts (to *do something which will now never be done*) for the sake of his family, that I wept bitterly in his presence. It hurt and distressed him much; he begged me to leave off: "O mother! Mother! Mother! Don't, don't – It has been a terrible struggle [to let go of his family and the world] – do let me go!" When, hungry for the love-tokens which were so freely given in health, I pleaded for one tender word to cheer my heart, when he should be gone, I pleaded in vain. He could not give what my heart so ached for: not because his affections are dead, for when I lay my hand on his (left hand) he will clasp and press it fondly; if I lay down beside him in the bed as he wishes me to do every night, he will put his *one* arm round me, and press me to his bosom and kiss me. But he says "It is all I can do to keep myself steady."

Oct. 7th. Husband slept all night. When I rose at daylight, he was awake. I asked him if he knew me. He quickly reached out his hand, caught mine and pressed it, then put his arm around me, drew me to him in a loving clasp, repeating the pressure three times and tried to kiss me! Such was his last loving farewell to the wife of his bosom! (Early diaries)

Joel passed away later that same afternoon. Sarah's diary became an outlet for her grief.

Nov. 7th, 1886. O, the days are so lonely and the nights so dreary! ... I have never really mourned for my dear departed: I cannot mourn for him, knowing so well that it "is well with him." Asleep in Jesus, blessed sleep! From which none ever wakes to weeping but the bereaved heart will sometimes yearn for its natural mate. The little ones' kisses are very sweet, and their love is very cheering, but they have not that soul-thrilling depth and power that was in their father's kiss, when with his arm about me or my hand clasped in his he drew me to him, and his face would glow with love and his eye beam with tenderness! ... How can I realize that I shall never enjoy this happiness again?

Sarah's family seems to have to rallied round her in those early days of widowhood. Despite her ideological differences with Sarah, Martha, who had lost her own husband only a few years earlier, was remarkably supportive to Sarah and her children and seems to have made a particular effort to be with them whenever she could: "Oct. 31. We were pleasantly surprised by a flying visit from sister Martha Towers and Stanley her second boy. They only stayed a few hours, and when they went took Emery home with them. Alice is to go the last of the week to take her place in a newly opened tailor's shop. O then I shall be lonely! Her presence and company have done much to cheer these first weeks of widowhood, for she is a happy-hearted girl, singing most of the time, almost all day long like a bird in spring" (Early diaries).

Joel's death became the catalyst for dramatic change in the lives of the Craig family. Despite his strong support of women's rights and especially of the reform dress, Joel's rigid views and his inherent pessimism, born of a lifetime of disappointment and bad luck and exacerbated by a stubborn pride that prevented him from accepting anything that smacked of "charity," seem to have militated against any new family ventures. With his death, forces already at play were released.

Chapter Four

Seeking a New Home: New Jersey and the West

Sarah Craig's longing for a better life in a congenial community had never died. However, after Joel's sudden death it was transmuted into a more pressing need for *any* kind of community where she could earn enough to raise her children and offer them better opportunities. She had long wanted to leave New Brunswick for greener pastures, and her restlessness intensified in the months following her husband's death: "When I think of the place and my relations to it, I seem to be drifting in a drifting landscape, where there is neither bottom nor shore – nothing to attach myself to, or fix my mind upon. I feel as if I could hardly bear to live here, and still less bear to leave the place where we spent so many happy days together" (Early diaries, 7 November 1886).

Christmas and New Year's were particularly hard. Sarah found the absence of her older children painful. Albert had joined the Salvation Army just before his father's death and was now working for that organization in far-off Ontario; Alice was employed in the tailoring shop in St Stephen; and Frank was also in St Stephen, having been hired at Ganong's chocolate factory. Thus there were three fewer mouths to feed at home, but Sarah was "keenly conscious of the breaks in our family circle" (Early diaries, 2 January

1887). The Craigs had a tradition of singing together, especially around Christmas: "We had a sweet family choir when we were together; we will never sing all together again on earth! .... we sang together an hour this evening, selecting many of the old favorites, but the music was not like we had when the father and older children were present: Alice's sweet soprano voice, Albert with his deep bass, [Frank] Ernest accompanying; while their father would sometimes sing bass and sometimes soprano as rich and clear as any woman in the land! O, I have not felt so lonely and strangely before" (Early diaries, 2 January 1887).

The older children were managing to send home some of their wages, but it was never enough; the post office, which had brought in a little income, had been swiftly removed from the Craig home after Joel's death (for reasons never fully explained to Sarah), and there were debts to be paid at the general store. And to make matters worse, she and her children were still living in Mrs Craig's house; Joel had never managed to finish the home he had planned to build for his family. The result was a profound sense of dislocation: "I cannot plan or hardly think of anything ahead; everything seems cut loose and drifting away and I with it into the unknown. On every side, I meet his unfinished work, physical or mental now alas! never to be finished" (Early diaries, 2 January 1887).

This feeling of being adrift may have clouded her judgment and led to misunderstanding and anguish. For a few months in 1887 she thought that J.W. Stevenson, an old friend and long-time neighbour in the community who was one of Joel's cousins, was courting her. He is mentioned often in the diaries over the years as a stalwart friend of the family, someone who helped Joel with numerous building projects. He even sat up with Joel during his final illness. But his sympathetic words and gestures in the months after her husband's death were easily misinterpreted by the grieving widow:

> J.W.S. called this evening. He was here last Monday too ... A romance is coming into my life, filling up the aching void caused by the sudden removal of the lover of my youth – a romance as sweet and tender as the sweet story of love first told in the garden of Eden! I have another lover! My husband's dear friend and cousin J.W. Stevenson, who was my legal adviser after my husband's death – a noble, Christian gentleman, always kind and deferential, comes to me now in the tender guise and manner of a lover! How kind my Father is to me! My heart grows young in the sunshine of this new love. (Early diaries, 9 May 1887)

Sarah reached desperately for this new romance. However, she may have misunderstood Stevenson's intentions, since her diary entries suggest that he was not altogether aware of how his affectionate words and body language might be misconstrued.

> July 8th Last evening I had a call from my dear friend J.W.S., with whom I spent an hour *very* pleasantly in affectionate intercourse. His last call left me very unhappy; I had tried to ascertain his real sentiments toward myself, (not of course by direct question) and he not understanding me, answered in a way to make me think I had been the dupe of my own foolish fancy ... But last night he was the same kind, loving friend, only more affectionate than before, so full of tender confidences and caressing ways and withal so gentlemanly,

that I forgot my embarrassment over the former scene, and
the bitterness succeeding it, and bade him "Good night" in
a happy frame of mind; and knelt and thanked my loving
Father for the blessing of love! (Early diaries)

Sarah's happiness was not to last. Perhaps Stevenson's feelings
changed, or perhaps he had never had romance in mind in the
first place; the true reasons seem not to have been clear to her.
Given that her diaries for most of 1887 are filled with notes about
letters exchanged with reformers and her various plans for moving west, Stevenson must have been aware that she might not
remain in New Brunswick for long. If he had any intention of proposing marriage, he must have known that he needed to move
quickly. In the end, it all came to nothing.

Oct. 5, 1887. Had quite a long call from J.W.S. During a long
and pleasant interview, in answer to some searching questions which I felt I had a right under the circumstances to
ask, he disclaimed all intentions towards me, except those
of intimate and privileged friendship! Thus this hope, over
which I have longed and wept and prayed so much, has been
withdrawn. O, may he never know the bitter anguish, the
cruel heartache this fond, foolish love-dream has cost me,
and will cost me, thro' coming years! (Early diaries)

Stevenson must surely have realized that marriage to Sarah
would entail taking on the support of a large family which included
several children under the age of ten, two of whom (Esther and
Florence) were very small. Moreover, he may have had second
thoughts about marrying a woman who still insisted on wearing

the reform dress. In the midst of what she construed as his court-
ship of her, she made these comments in her diary after receiving
a letter from a dress reformer with whom she had recently re-
established contact: "Many think that *now I am a widow*, I will
change my style, with a view to sometime getting a husband; but
they do not know the stuff I am made of, or the principles on which
my eccentric style is based. If any man wants to make me his wife,
he must take me as I am in my 'Freedom suit,' untrammelled, and
unfettered by fashion. I cannot sacrifice my freedom and my principles even to Love. By so doing I should wrong him and myself
too" (Early diaries, 25 May 1887).

Stevenson may have quietly counted the cost and deemed it
too high, but it seems more likely that he was simply unaware of
Sarah's feelings. Her last mention of him, in November 1887, just
before the family left for New Jersey, states, "He is just the same
kind friend, his manner unchanged, claiming the same lover-like
privileges, as before, quite unconscious how hard it is for my heart
to feel 'hitherto shalt come and no further.'" It is possible that
Sarah had been misreading him all along. At any rate, without any
commitment from Stevenson, she obviously felt that she had no
future in New Brunswick and needed to seek a better life elsewhere.

What seems to have kept Sarah going during these first months
of confusion and bereavement were the contacts she had made or
revived during the renewed interest in the colony plan during the
last two years before Joel's death. These included some of the most
famous American dress reformers, such as Mary E. Tillotson, who
had presided over a revival of interest in dress reform in the 1870s,
founding the American Free Dress League and promoting what
she called the "Science costume."

Yesterday I received a letter from Mary E. Tillotson of
Vineland, NJ, a Dress-reformer to whom I wrote a few weeks
ago. She sends her picture at the head of a column of testi-
monials of Dress-reformers clipped from a California paper.
It shows her beautiful "Science costume," a coat dress reach-
ing to the knee, pantaloons and boots protecting the limbs
and feet. A white bosom and tie finish at the neck. Her letter
is very refreshing. She is one of but two Dress-reformers
left in that city which once she says gave that cause the best
chance of any place she knew. She is 70 years of age but is still
an active worker and writer in the cause. Bids me not be dis-
couraged – stick to my dress and keep it on my girls! (Early
diaries, 22 May 1887)

As the year went on, these contacts began to bear some fruit. A
series of entries in Sarah's diary indicate a flurry of correspondence with old friends and new:

June 29, 1887. Received a long letter from Mrs Harman [the
dress reformer from Kokomo, Indiana], containing various
suggestions on the subject of my moving my family; gave
me several addresses to write to for information &c.
July 20th. 1887. Received a letter from one of the facculty
of the new Hygienic College; also one from Dr Gifford of
Kokomo Ind. Dr G. would like to have me and my family
go out there this fall and take charge of his fruit farm, and
garden, and work in the "Home" at intervals! Perhaps this
is the chance – the opening – I have been looking for.
July 24th More letters from the West – one from a lady in
New Jersey, on the chance for settling there; another from a

gentleman in Missouri telling of a young colony in Arkansas, the description of which I like very much but it is too far away for our present means. One thing disturbs me: it is, that among the best and most radical and necessary reforms, there is, in many cases, mixed so much *rank infidelity*! Be it mine to hold to Christ our true Head wherever I go or whatever I do.

Aug. 6th News from Florida! A little Colony of reformers at Grahamville wish me to join them. Pleasant place and good society; but very little chance for a woman to earn a living for herself and family. The letter was from two dress-reformers – sisterly, affectionate epistles; but they are Spiritualists, and seem to set very little store by the Bible or the religion of Jesus Christ. I must speak a word for my dear Captain when I write to them.

In these entries, Sarah points to a problem that would almost certainly have undermined her chances of fitting in with a real "colony of reformers": her unwillingness to join a group that did not completely share her own beliefs. In these diary entries it is her Christian beliefs that are the issue, but it seems likely that any ideological differences could have undermined her willingness to get along with members of a large group.

Nevertheless, this barrage of correspondence eventually did bring an opening. Hearing of Sarah's widowhood and her need to find a new home, one of the old correspondents and prospective colonists from the 1860s, James Allen, wrote to offer the Craigs a place in New Jersey. He and his wife were apparently travelling and lecturing on health issues and needed someone to farm their land for them. Their current tenant, Mrs Zimmerman, was leaving and they did not want the house to stand empty. Having considered the other offers, most of which were from communities too far away, Sarah writes in her diary: "So we think we will take up with Allen's offer. I will write next mail for his exact terms: he says his terms will be *very easy*, and liberal. He wants his place taken care of while he is away; and he wants to get a number of progressive people together to form the nucleus of a co-operative or Communistic Home, somewhat on the plan suggested by my husband and me over twenty years ago. How delightful if the seed we two then planted should bear good fruit, and I and my children live to pluck it" (Early diaries, 5 October 1887).

Sarah and her family spent the next busy few weeks selling their goods and packing what they could take with them. A bill of $50.00 had long been waiting for payment at the local grocery store, and other debts of Joel's also remained, so there was little profit to be realized from the sale of their property. Sarah's diary entries communicate her difficult situation: she needed every dollar she could get, and yet the pressure to sell at any price was intense.

Oct. 17th 1887. I went to see R. McKinney, with a view to making arrangements about the Bill, standing against us on his Ledger. He said he had been thinking of consulting a lawyer about selling the place (*our place*) to get his money out of it! He has not acted on this idea yet, but will when he goes to St Stephen. This looks rather hard, but I don't see any way to help it.

Oct. 18th. Two men came about noon to look at our hay. Did not like the hay – not coarse enough for horses – but they got to looking at the tools, (which had been gathered into the

great chest awaiting the Auction, notices for which we are
having put up now) and Frank, tempted by a little money,
and without coming to consult me, sold the bulk of the tools
much too cheaply – for just about *half the value* we had put
upon them. When they came down – they had been looking
at the cows before – one of them bought the young cow, and
gave me $11.00; I could have got $12.00 if I had been sharp,
but I have heard so much lately about cows being so cheap
(from 10 to 15 dollars) that I was afraid if I asked a *price* I
would get nothing.

    After they left, Mr. Boone from Oak Bay came and after
looking at things a while, offered $15.00 for the other cow,
and to leave her with us till Nov. 1st. I was loth to take it, but
Frank and Alice both persuaded me it was better than another dollar *and give her right up.* The milk and butter are
worth a dollar a week. So both cows are sold. (Early diaries)

The Craigs held their auction on 1 November 1887, disposing of
most of what was saleable and some things that they had not
thought of parting with as well. Unfortunately, Sarah complains
that "when I was not present to bid, some things were sold shame-
fully cheap." But other items fetched a fair price, and the family
made more than $30.00 from the sale.

    Amidst these busy preparations for the journey, Sarah's doubts
about this momentous decision to leave the only home she had
ever known persisted. However much she longed to take her children to a "new country," facing the unknown was very hard: "Oct.
27th I cannot begin to do justice to what I am passing thro' on
paper. I want to do what is the Lord's will – to give up my own;
but I am in an agony of doubt some times lest it is all wrong that

we are doing just now when I had rather decide to stay at home. I seem to hear the command 'Go forward!'" (Early diaries). The sale of the land was the biggest issue, given the size of the out-standing debt. In the end, the property was left in the hands of three trustees, rather than being sold outright; they were to cut and sell cordwood and lumber from the land until the $50.00 bill was paid off. There is no further comment in the surviving diaries regarding what was ultimately done with the Craig property. Nevertheless, Joel's mother seems to have remained in the house, having secured a promise of care from the "overseers of the poor" in the area (who are not mentioned elsewhere in Sarah's diaries) to support her for the rest of her days (Early diaries, 16 February 1887). She bid farewell to Sarah and her grandchildren with great sadness. She would keep in touch with her daughter-in-law by mail, and over the next few years Sarah mentions in her diary that Mrs Craig had sent small amounts of money in payment for a bureau that Sarah had left behind. She also says that Mrs Craig missed her grandchildren terribly. In later years Martha's son Emery often spent a week or two with "Grannie Craig" helping her to plant her garden, always reporting that she was "very lonely." Her death is not recorded; she may have passed away dur-ing the family's stay in Ontario.

With the furniture and tools sold and the debt on the land taken care of, the whole family then set off on their journey into an unknown future:

Nov. 6. 1887. Before sunrise the team drove up – a span and beg hayrack – into which our chests & boxes were piled, leav-ing a space in the middle which was filled with bedding and loose quilts as a nest for the children ... We had a pretty cold ride, and were glad of a ... good warm fire when we got here to Mother's. But a good dinner made us all feel better ... Our dear friends were glad and sorry all at once – glad to see us, and sorry to say farewell, but hopeful that we may be going for the better ... Well! In the morning we must take leave of all these dear ones, and of our native land! And be borne away to a new country and untried scenes, to cast our lot among strangers. But our God is there too, and if He is with us we need fear nothing. (Early diaries)

Thus Sarah set off, with all of her children except for Albert, the oldest, who was still working with the Salvation Army in Ontario. There seems to have been no question of leaving Alice behind to work in the shop in St Stephen; Sarah clearly hoped for better opportunities for her daughter in New Jersey, and besides, she needed her help with the younger children. Little Florence was only three at the time, while Esther, whom Sarah once described as a "witching, winning little fairy, full of sweet loving wiles and wilfulness" (Early diaries, 14 March 1886), was five. Lucy was ten, but not yet strong enough to help with the heavy household chores. And although Joel Bonney (whom Sarah often refers to as J.B. or "Bonney") was now fourteen, he suffered from rheumatism and headaches and was not strong. Charlie, intellectually very bright and with a photographic memory, was not physically strong either. Nine-year-old Willie was the most energetic of the boys, but too young to take on much responsibility. So Alice and Frank were the mainstays of the family.

The journey by boat to Ancora, New Jersey, via Boston, where the whole family was able to see some of the sights of the city, and then on to New York, was interesting but uneventful. Sarah's diary account describes the trip in detail with a tourist's keen eye, despite her cares as a mother herding a large brood of children on and off boats and trains.

> We watched the lights on Brooklyn Bridge, till the gleaming arch swept over our heads, just as we caught sight of a single light in the distance, which we soon recognized as Bartholdi's colossal statue "Liberty enlightening the world." How proudly we gazed on these wonders of human handicraft! things we never once thought of seeing when we left home … But Steam, the roaring, snorting, rushing giant, waits for no man: the ferry took us from New York to Jersey City, whence another ride on the cars bro't us to Philadelphia, where we waited some hours in another noisy waiting room, then a ride in the horse-cars, another ferry across the Delaware river to Camden, then 25 miles on the train bro't us to Ancora, our destination. Half a mile walk, thro' the wet night over sand which felt like melted snow under our feet found us at Mr. Allen's door. (Early diaries, 11 November 1887)

Sarah and her children had arrived in a very interesting part of the United States. Ancora was close to Vineland, New Jersey, a town that had been created by a man with his own utopian dreams. It had been developed and settled by a wealthy and ideal- istic developer, Charles Kline Landis, in the 1860s.[1] He intended it to be a "planned agricultural community"[2] that would also be alcohol free.[3] Landis, who had already established the settler town of Hammonton on the new railway line that connected the area with Atlantic City, began buying up more acreage with the intention of establishing his "grand plans for a colony on an even larger scale" than Hammonton, which had by this time become a prosperous fruit-producing community.[4] Hearing of a new rail line that was being built to run between Glassboro and Millville, he purchased numerous tracts of wooded land there and began to plan his ideal agricultural town. He described his agenda as "to found a place which ... might be the abode of happy, prosperous and beautiful homes; establish the best of schools; also manufactories, and different industries and churches of different denominations; in short, all things essential to the prosperity of mankind ... that the home of every man of reasonable industry might be made a sanctuary of happiness, and an abode of beauty, no matter how poor he might be."[5]

Indeed, this settlement seems to have been a larger version of the nineteenth-century utopian colony, with its emphasis on self-sufficiency and the growing of abundant crops. Landis may have known about the Oneida Community or Brook Farm, both colonies established earlier in the century with similar goals of self-sufficiency. In Vineland, however, the surplus produce was to be shipped north to be sold in Philadelphia and New York for profit, not consumed by the local people. And the town was strictly regulated in order to maintain the focus on growing fruit and vegetables; indeed, Vineland remains an agricultural area to this day. When Sarah and her family arrived in New Jersey, this settlement had been established for less than thirty years, yet it was already a prosperous community that had attracted a number of eccentrics and radical reformers of various types. She writes, "Vineland is a lovely place: the streets are broad, with rows of trees all along each side, edging the side walks" (Early diaries, 30 October 1888). Those rows of shade trees had been mandated by Landis himself.

However, when they first arrived in New Jersey Sarah and her children had more immediate concerns. They received a warm welcome from Mrs Zimmerman, the tenant, but Sarah soon found that the Allen property was not all she had hoped for. It was immediately clear that the farm was too small and in too poor a condition to support her and her eight children. The grounds were pretty and studded with trees and flower beds, but it was not as large a property as she had expected: "there is a small orchard at one end and 150 grape vines at the other. It is a rather pretty place, very retired tho' quite near the neighbors, but too small, or rather in too poor a state of tillage to support a family like ours. 12 acres of land if we could do with it as we would, and had means to live thro' the winter, could be made in a year so it would support us; but it is not our own, and we must turn at once to solving the problem of bread and butter!" (Early diaries, 11 November 1887).

Once again, poverty frustrated Sarah's plans. Arriving in November made the situation worse, since it would clearly be months before any crops could be planted and the orchard trees bear fruit. Moreover, having spent all the capital raised from the sale of their few belongings in New Brunswick to travel to New Jersey, the family had no cash with which to buy supplies to begin farming. Sarah writes in her diary: "Jan. 1, 1888. In a letter from Mrs Allen, they offer us all we can raise on the place this year, they furnishing manure, etc., if we will go to work on it and bring it into a state to raise something worthwhile. But with no capital to start with, or rather to live on in the meantime, we can't do *that* just now."

Furthermore, the revived relationship with the absent Allens got off to a rocky start, since Sarah had not handled the arrangements in the way that they had stipulated:

Mr Allen, in his first letter, seemed surprised, and not altogether pleased, at our coming here without first paying the
sum of $25.00, which he had named in an "Agreement" he
sent for me to sign and return; which by the way I never
signed or returned, because I could not raise the money ...
and because I did not want to pay money on uncertainties.
At the same time I knew Mrs Zimmerman intended to leave;
and he wanted someone in his house – it would be better,
tenanted, than empty – so I came; believing that once here,
I could find *another* chance, if this one did not suit me, or
I it. (Early diaries, 1 January 1888)

To make matters worse, the people of this community were what
Sarah termed "generally Spiritualists and infidels – outspoken
Heaven-daring infidels" (Early diaries, 11 November 1887) and consequently far from her notions of a community of "congenial
minds." New Jersey was not, after all, the Promised Land she had
hoped it would be.

As time went on, however, she became good friends with some
of these people and got to know others in the Christian circles that
she joined. By March 1888 she was able to write: "Have made the
acquaintance of many excellent people – some Christians, some
spiritualists, some Infidels, many of them highly cultured and re-
fined; we enjoy the society of the Christians and others too very
much, and endeavor to 'let our light be seen' to hold up the ban-
ner of the Cross on all occasions." Her children, too, were making
friends and settling into their new community.

Nevertheless, the financial problems that had prompted the ex-
odus from New Brunswick in the first place persisted in this new

home. The eldest son with them, Frank, had found some work but not steady employment; the next few months saw him trying his hand at everything from labouring jobs to painting photographs. Joel, now fifteen, was hired by various people in the district to do chores. Sarah and Alice both earned a few dollars a week doing laundry for people, and Alice began housekeeping for neighbourhood women in order to earn more. However, Sarah's assessment in March, after three months in their new home, was realistic, albeit determinedly upbeat:

> March 1st 1888. We have earned our expenses, but have *nothing ahead*. Have had plenty of good wholesome food, of very nice quality, and been able to buy milk, most of the time, but sugar is cheapest, and we have it right along. I have only bought *two loads* of wood. May have to buy another. We are all well and hearty, and happy as we know how to be. I feel much more at home and not half so homesick as I did the last year I spent at home, where all around me, indoors or out, was something to remind me of the dear departed, and his desperate tho' unsuccessful struggles to make a *comfortable* home for his family. I have "let go of the past" and "look with hope into the future." (Early diaries)

On 13 March Sarah received a letter from Mr and Mrs Allen "expressing the wish that we would stay on their place all summer and work it; we can have all we can raise. They seem very kind, and if Our Father does not open another door for us very soon, I shall take it for granted that His purpose is for us to stay here." She wrote back to accept their offer, and the family began pruning fruit trees and planting early seeds, in preparation for the farming season. It is worth noting that there was no further mention by the Allens of establishing a "communistic" farm on their property; perhaps they too had realized that the place was too small to sustain more than one family.

Sarah's diary entries for the summer of 1888 show that the family supported themselves through a combination of berry picking, housework, and occasional chores while they farmed the Allens' property as well as they could and waited for the fruit to ripen. The Allens' home was located in an area where there was an abundance of fruit and berries to be picked, and they often got work on other people's farms. Although Sarah and her children did not earn a great deal, it was often much more than they had been accustomed to in New Brunswick. Nevertheless, the heavy toll that "working out" exacted on Alice, in particular, began to be apparent. On 9 September 1888 Sarah writes in her diary of Alice's illness after a particularly exhausting stint working at another woman's house and of her own application of water-cure methods of treatment in her daughter's case:

> We are coming thro' a strange and far from pleasant experience now … Some 12 days ago, while neither strong nor well, she did a pretty large washing and got dinner, and then walked to camp-meeting, over two miles, and walked back late in the evening. Next morning Mrs H. took suddenly ill and fell on the floor. Alice helped lift her – she is a great, heavy, swinish woman, and has been nearly helpless for over two years with paralysis – and then waited upon her all day and the next night. In the morning she sent for me: I went and took charge, and at night Nettie Wood bro't Alice home to rest. If I had come with her, she would not have been so ill

– I could have assisted Nature's remedial efforts before so
much of the system became involved. But she and I both
hoped that rest would bring her round again; and Mrs H.
had to have *somebody*, so I staid sorely against my wishes
till Tuesday night (I went on Saturday).

When Mrs H.'s own doctor called on Alice, he realized she was
sicker than anyone had thought; he even suggested that she had
come down with typhoid fever (which turned out not to be the
case). But this alarming diagnosis prompted Mrs H.'s family to
engage another housekeeper, and Sarah came home to treat Alice
herself. When she arrived at the house, everyone was in bed and so
she retired, only to be wakened by her daughter's condition.

Alice grew very feverish and restless, and finally began to get
delirious. I rose, and having no other appliances at hand,
dipped a cloth in cold water and sponged her head thoroly,
then her spine, then lightly wrung a cloth out of cold water
and laid it the whole length of the spine and up over the
cerebellum, covering it with a dry towel, sponged the rest of
the body, tucked her up and she fell asleep and slept till
morning sweetly. In the forenoon I gave her a [wet-sheet]
pack, which refreshed her much. And so I am keeping it up,
day and night; I take a kettle of hot water to the bedroom at
night for tepid pouring head bath, which is the best anodyne
for her sleeplessness. (Early diaries, 9 September 1888)

No diagnosis other than sheer physical overexertion is suggested
in Sarah's account. Alice did recover from this episode, but had a
relapse soon after and needed more care and rest. This recurrence

should have been seen as a warning that she could not keep up the pace of such heavy housework, which inevitably included washing large amounts of heavy clothes and bedding. The constant need to fetch water from pumps made a young woman's work physically demanding and potentially harmful. And despite the strenuous nature of this labour, the pay was minimal: Sarah and Alice could expect to be paid only 50 or 75 cents for a washing that took the whole day to complete.

Although Sarah does not make much of the topic in her diaries, this part of New Jersey harboured a number of dress and health reformers. On 16 April 1888 she notes that she met Mrs Lucas, "a doctor ... of the Hygienic school" who was treating a woman in the neighbourhood. Mrs Lucas introduced Sarah to two very famous dress reformers, Mary E. Tillotson (with whom Sarah had corresponded while still in New Brunswick) and Susan Pecker Fowler. In her diary Sarah writes, "At last I have paid a visit to Mrs Lucas at Newfield. I took Esther with me, left home Friday, and took cars at Winslow for Vineland, arrived there, found Mrs Tillotson a thorogoing dress reformer, who was very much pleased to see me, kept me to dinner, after which she took me to see Miss Susan Fowler, another champion of the short dress with whom we staid till dusk, then returned to Mrs T.'s to spend the night" (30 October 1888).

Mary Tillotson was one of the original dress reformers. After suffering from dyspepsia (severe indigestion) for a number of years, she had been encouraged by her husband to try wearing the reform dress. In her published history of the dress-reform movement she writes that she was rapidly cured after she abandoned her corsets.[6] By 1864 her marriage had broken down, and she had moved with her son to Vineland, where she purchased a house and property during the first blossoming of the settlement as a planned agricultural community. Here she established a garden and vineyard and "took pride in her self-sufficiency."[7] She wore her "Science costume" (as she called it) full-time as she worked around her farm and on various projects in the community. She continued to wear the reform outfit for the rest of her life and was at one point jailed in Newark, New Jersey,[8] and on another occasion in Watkins, New York, for walking the streets wearing pants.[9] On both occasions she was quickly released, but the incidents highlighted the continuing hostility toward women who dared to dress in a radical style.

Susan Fowler was another dress reformer who ran her own farm in Vineland. She had settled in the town shortly after it was founded and was one of many inhabitants with alternative lifestyles and controversial ideas.[10] At one point she "shocked Vineland residents in her day parading down Landis Avenue in a tunic and bloomers or trousers."[11] According to a 1904 newspaper report, Fowler had initially adopted the version of the reform costume worn by women in the Oneida Community, which was quite feminine.[12] However, a photo of her later in life shows her wearing the more masculine "Science costume" favoured by Mary Tillotson. Like Tillotson and other dress reformers, Fowler was also an outspoken advocate for women's rights, arguing that she ought not to be required to pay taxes if she, as a woman, was denied the vote. To make her point, in November 1868 "she and 171 other determined Vineland women ... voted in the election," having fashioned their own ballot box out of two blueberry crates.[13] She was instrumental in bringing nationally known speakers such as Susan B. Anthony and Elizabeth Cady Stanton to headline rallies for women's suffrage in the area.[14] Fowler had never married and had always worked her farm on her own, but in 1904 she apparently realized, at the age of eighty, that she could not continue the farm work by herself, and she advertised for male help. She was in the news again a few months later when she prepared to marry a forty-six-year-old man who had answered her advertisement and proposed marriage to her. She was dubbed "Vineland's oddest character" by the *Brookfield Courier*, which particularly noted that she had made her wedding trousseau in the reform style.[15]

When Sarah Craig met these two women in 1888, Tillotson was seventy and Fowler sixty-five. Both had been extremely active in social and political movements for decades and were among those few determined women who still wore the reform costume. By this point, Tillotson had published four books on the subject of women's dress, along with many articles in reformist papers.[16] She is mentioned several other times in Sarah's diaries – as a guest at Christmas celebrations that December, for instance – and she seems to have become a friend. In fact, Sarah apparently stayed overnight at her house on a number of occasions. But the dress-reform issue is seldom discussed in the diaries during this time.

It is possible that Sarah saw Mary Tillotson's situation as a single woman of some means, supporting herself on her own farm and vineyard, as the anomaly it surely was, and realized that she could not hope to replicate it in her own life. The prosperous farmers of Vineland owned their own properties, something that Sarah could never hope to do. Moreover, Tillotson was a spiritualist, like Mrs Zimmerman, and was thus not attuned to Sarah's personal Christian faith. As well, by the late 1880s the dress-reform movement had largely run out of steam, and many health reformers had turned their attention to other issues, such as women's suffrage and temperance reform.[17] Indeed, Mrs Lucas encouraged Sarah to come to the Woman's Christian Temperance Union, which they joined together. It seems that, by necessity, Sarah's reformist energies were once again channelled in that direction. Certainly, there is no further mention of employment possibilities for her children at Our Home on the Hillside in Dansville, New York, an institution that had also run its course as more modern medical practices finally took the place of water-cure therapy. It would seem that, having finally escaped to a community where there were a number of congenial reformist friends, Sarah was forced to concede that there was no road forward for her ideal "colony."

There were some compensations, however. She certainly appreciated the milder climate and the natural beauty of the place, and she and the children clearly made many friends in Ancora, Vineland, Hammonton, and Newfield, attending church meetings, picnics, and other social events. Some of their new friends generously gave them gifts of used clothing and kitchen utensils. Moreover, crops could be planted much earlier than in New Brunswick, and berry picking began in May. Spring blooms were abundant even in April. In May 1888 Sarah writes in her diary: "What a lovely country! For a month the dooryards have been gay with purple moss-pink, yellow forsythia (great shrubs hung with golden bells clear to the ground) crimson flowering quince and blush-white almond with its lovely plumes and clusters of miniature roses with the snow-white bridal flower between, of which, shaking a branch, the tiny petals fell in a great shower like a snow storm in NB. All these have faded, and been replaced by others; the orchards have bloomed and shed their bloom ... and our garden seeds &c are coming up well." (Early diaries, 20 May 1888)

The family continued to cobble together a living of sorts, but doing so required the involvement of all the older members, including Lucy, who was only eleven years old.

Dec. 5th, 1888: An old lady who is very lame sent me word that she wanted Lucy to help her. Lucy did not want to go; but as it was the first word of work, we all urged her. I took her to see the lady Sunday; and as the man wanted the boys to husk, she came back and went with them next morning. They could not work as the man was too sick to get things ready, so they came home, and about 2 P.M. Lucy came home too. I asked her why she came – if she cried so much Mrs W. sent her home? She owned that it was so! Bonney is working there today; and Charlie is taking his first lessons in the Newfield printing office. He is in high spirits – was up before day, he and Bonney ate their meal, took their dinner, in their pockets, and started for their work in the grey light. Charlie worked 3 days [but] the man did not want him: he earned 50 cts, and Bonney got $1,05 for his work. (Early diaries)

February 1889 brought some developments, as the boys found work in various local industries; but there was still no sure way forward.

Feb. 26th. Frank is holding up his head bravely, tho' for the months he has earned very little but his board and spent his summer's savings trying to get started in what promised to be a paying business; then he spent two months working for his board at the poultry business, to learn that, as it pays well. The firm burst up, and as G.W. Elvins, his former employer,

had just lost a hand from his mill, Frank took the place behind the saw. He says he is bound to hoe his own row: if he
can't *help* us he will not *hinder* us; if he gets *blue* sometimes
it don't last long, and no body knows it but himself. It is a
good, cheering letter, and shows a strong manly spirit under
difficulties.

Apr. 23rd 1889. Sent Charlie again to inquire about work at
the Kane factory: result – Joel B. is taking his first lessons
there today. (Early diaries)

The most disheartening episode was the failed attempt to get
young Charlie trained in the printing business. Sarah's younger
brother, Edwin Jameson, was a printer in Buffalo, New York, and
had on more than one occasion helped out his sister financially.
In April 1889 he wrote to Sarah telling her of a possible opening
for Charlie in the printing office and asking if she would be able
to send the boy on the train "on a day's notice." She replied that
she could, but only if she had the boy's train fare, which she could
not afford to pay herself. Edwin wrote back, advising her to find
someone to loan her the money, which would be repaid as soon
as Charlie arrived in Buffalo. She did so, and Charlie left home on
9 May in high spirits. His early letters home indicate that he was
greatly enjoying his job as press and errand boy and was earning
$2.00 a week. However, by 9 June the bubble had burst. At first it
was not clear what had gone wrong, but as Sarah's diary for 16
June explains,

I got a letter from my brother, explaining the matter about
Charlie. He had not seen Charlie for *six years* and was much

disappointed at his *small* and *slender* appearance. He learned to work the press by *foot*, and tend it, but when they started it *by steam* he (being a half-sick with a cold just then) was not quite spry enough to feed it – and they only gave him the one chance to try. Edwin found him another place, where he worked three days and was dismissed because he "seemed to be stupid," as no doubt he was just then. He lost another place by refusing to bring whiskey. As yet no other chance has opened for him. He writes too, and seems to think he will come home as soon as the means can be got. I am disappointed; but it is all in the Lord's hands.

Problems with physical weakness would continue to dog Charlie all his life. It is possible that he and his brother Joel, who also remained sickly, had suffered the most from the constant lack of proper nutrition in the household during their crucial years of growth. At any rate, given that Charlie had always shown an interest in printing, much like his uncle Edwin (who had helped set the type for the *Car of Progress* when he was a child), this setback must have been more of a blow than Sarah admits in her diary. The printing business was one of the few sectors of employment for men where skill rather than simple physical strength was required, and she must have seen this opportunity for one of her sons as a breakthrough. But it was not to be.

Sarah's diaries break off before the conclusion of the New Jersey episode and remain silent for some twelve years, until she takes up her pen again in 1902. However, her youngest daughter Florence, who typed up her memoir in the 1960s, fills in some of the gaps. It seems that the older children eventually found paying work in factories in the area (a glass factory, in Frank's case) and the younger girls, Esther and Florence, got some rudimentary schooling. Albert and Frank both married.

But certainly the most traumatic event must have been the death of Alice, that "happy-hearted girl" of whom Sarah once wrote that she was "singing most of the time, almost all day long like a bird in spring" as she went about her household tasks (Early diaries, 31 October 1886). Alice had faithfully kept the family going, "working out" and sending her wages home when she could, and cheerfully helping her mother whenever needed. For most of 1888 she seems to have found steady employment in Vineland doing housework for one family, although there is a brief reference to her working in a shop there later on (Sarah does not specify what kind of shop this was). In May that year Sarah writes, "Alice came over and spent the evening with us. I miss her *so much*: she is so sweet naturally, and so strong and full of grace spiritually, she is a great help and support to me."

Florence describes the tragic events of 1893 in her additions to Sarah's memoir:

Lucy, working in a house where the kitchen floor was very cold and draughty that winter, got her feet badly frostbitten, and had to come home. Alice thought she could "fill in" while Lucy's feet got better; but it was too much for her. Think she was there only two weeks. The pump ... was *very hard* to pump; and it caused haemorrhage from the lungs; so she came home. I shall never forget that night. She opened the door and leaned against the door-jamb, her handkerchief to her mouth. Mother, looking up, startled, quickly grasped the situation; got Alice to the lounge, and did what could be done at the time. (Memoir, part 2, 43)

Florence adds no further details about Alice's diagnosis or about the treatment that she received. Given the family's poverty and Sarah's views on conventional medicine, it seems unlikely that she was treated by an allopathic physician. In fact, this condition, known as haemoptysis, is rarely described outside of tuberculosis. Mary S. Gove (later Mary Gove Nichols) was said to have suffered from the condition as a young woman after some "arduous labours" but recovered.[18] There is a chance that Alice had "congenital lung malformation of the blood vessels in the bronchi" or a congenital heart disease, which could have led to heart failure when worsened with exertion, resulting in an "acute hemorrhagic pulmonary edema."[19] Trall discusses several types of "bleeding from the lungs" in his *Hydropathic Encyclopedia*, but in almost all cases the treatment calls for keeping the patient quiet, sipping cold water, and swallowing small ice cubes.[20] Without modern diagnostic methods such as X-rays, it would have been virtually impossible to determine the cause. Sarah most likely tried every remedy at her disposal, but to no avail.

Florence concludes her account: "But after twelve weeks' suffering, with the best of care that could be given, our darling sister passed on to the 'green fields and shining angels' she told us she saw shortly before, on the evening of April 18, 1893 ... Lucy's feet having got well some time before this, she was back at work but said she'd like to cut her feet off!" (Memoir, part 2, 43). This heartbreaking end to Alice's life at the age of twenty-six points to the severe limitations faced by poor nineteenth-century women with little formal education. They were often doomed to doing heavy housework in order to make a living in an era without widespread electricity or running water, and with no washing machines or dryers to ease the arduous task of laundering heavy clothing and bedding.

Although Sarah's diaries break off before the year of Alice's death, it is possible that this event was one of the reasons for her long silence. To watch her daughter suffer for four long months without being able to help her must have been devastating. Sarah had eloquently described the deaths of dear young children and then the passing of her beloved husband. But the loss of this adult daughter, so full of life and cheer and so indispensable to her, must have been a blow like no other. Silence may have been the only possible response. Women diarists of this era, Helen Buss notes, often found the experience of mourning inexpressible, beyond discourse, and thus explicit references to such events are often cursory or omitted from their diaries altogether.[21] Sarah's somewhat guarded reference to Alice's earlier illness as a "strange and far from pleasant experience" signals how unsettling the idea of losing her daughter must have been. To actually lose her was a tragedy beyond words. There is only one reference to Alice's death in Sarah's subsequent diaries, twenty-three years later: "June 26, 1916. This is our dear departed Alice's birth-day – her 49th anniversary. How Time passes!" (Later diaries). Obviously, Alice had never been forgotten.

By the time of Alice's death, the boys' prospects seem to have improved slightly. Florence notes that Charlie had moved to Buffalo in 1892 but does not say if he was employed again at Uncle Edwin's printing office or somewhere else. Frank was married and had found work in a factory in Bridgeton, New Jersey, and Will, one of the younger boys, was working at the iron works there; so the whole family moved to Bridgeton. Meanwhile, Albert, the Salvation Army officer, was living in Wyoming, a small town four miles north of Petrolia, in an agricultural area of southwestern Ontario near Sarnia. In the spring of 1894 he sent for Lucy to come and help his pregnant wife and for Joel to come and look for work there; so both young people went. The next few months saw preparations for another major family move, this time to Ontario. They made the journey in two stages because funds were lacking, stopping in Buffalo on the way for a visit with Edwin and his family and apparently for Charlie to join them. The end of 1894 saw the family – all but Frank – installed in Wyoming, squeezed into a very small house but finding employment in various places, including a woollen mill.

Thus closed the New Jersey chapter. Having brought her family to the state in hopes of joining or starting a "communistic farm," Sarah had been forced to concede that such a scheme was not viable for a large family with no capital. Unfortunately, her timing was off: if she had arrived ten years earlier, she might have benefited more from her contacts with famous dress reformers in the Vineland area, but by the 1880s the force of the movement was largely spent.

A cynical assessment of the New Jersey episode can be found in a letter from Uncle Edwin to Florence, dated 21 March 1935. Edwin had grown up during the first excitement of the colony scheme, and at the age of nine he had helped Joel set the type for the one and only issue of the *Car of Progress*. Yet his outsider's eye allowed him to see the follies of the search for utopia more clearly than his determined sister ever could. He wrote to Florence that "your mother was assured by the Allens and others that the whole family could *easily* earn a livelihood by picking fruit! What sort of fruit could be picked in winter was not specified." Edwin goes on to note in the same letter that the colony plan was only one among "a thousand of those Utopian schemes planned and nearly as many launched" in the nineteenth century. When he notes that nearly all such communities soon broke apart through "incompatibility," he highlights an issue that Sarah and Joel seem never to have considered in planning their community of strangers. He clearly also has in mind his older brother Isaac, who *did* move to the United States to join a colony in the 1860s and whom Edwin describes as "an inveterate 'joiner' of everything he could get near in socialistic schisms"; he was ultimately left "sour and bitter" by the failure of these communities to measure up to his ideals. If Sarah's dealings with the Allens in New Jersey afford any hints, the proposed "colony of reformers" was likely doomed to failure from the beginning. Nevertheless, the dream of a utopian community did have some positive long-term effects for her and her surviving children: it gave her both the contacts and the impetus to leave New Brunswick, where it seemed she would never have been able to prosper, and to embark on the gradual move westward that eventually resulted in her family's moderate success.

A few months after the move to Ontario, Sarah found employment keeping house and looking after four very young children for a farmer whose wife had been admitted to a mental hospital. By the time she left this job, Lucy was working in nearby Petrolia, and by 1896 the older boys were employed at stave mills in Enniskillen Township and Glen Rae, both near Wyoming. Florence managed to finish high school and then found work taking care of infant twins. However, from her notes about the next few years, it seems that the family was, once again, barely managing to

4.1 Sarah Craig and her children in Holmesdale, Ontario, in 1897

live day to day. Sarah and her two youngest girls, Esther and Florence, seem to have spent some years moving from one home to another, staying with Albert's family to help with his young children at first and then living in the farmer's house for almost a year. Eventually, the whole family moved into several log cabins clustered near the stave mill in Holmesdale, in Enniskillen Township, which they got rent free; these dwellings were adjacent to the forest but with enough cleared land to plant vegetables. A surviving photograph shows Sarah and her children in front of their log cabin (see figure 4.1).

By 1897 Charlie and Will had rejoined the family, and for a time all the young men were working in the stave mill. But this operation always closed for the winter and sometimes remained shut for months longer. In 1900 Albert and his family and Charlie moved further north to Midland, Ontario – Albert to work in a smelter and Charlie in a lumber mill. Albert was even able to buy a house there. But certainly by 1900 most family members were starting to look west to the prairies for further opportunities. Farmland in Ontario was too expensive for them, and prices in the west beckoned. This was just before the great wave of westward migration in the first decade of the twentieth century.[22] Cheerful pamphlets trumpeting the benefits of prairie living to potential settlers may have influenced their decision, but the Craigs were already predisposed to try anything that would enable them to own their own land.[23]

The frustration of these Ontario years may have contributed to the long hiatus in Sarah's diaries. Certainly, there is no sense from Florence's brief account that the family felt they were moving forward or making any headway in improving their fortunes. It seems strange that Sarah was able to keep writing her diaries for years while constantly bearing children and coping with a husband who was often ill, and yet abandoned writing them when her children were partly grown. Florence makes no comment on the possible reasons for her mother's silence; perhaps she simply did not know. But one wonders if Sarah saw her dream of finding an Eden for her family slipping away. Nevertheless, although she kept no diaries, she did write three contributions during this time for *The Jamesons in America*, the massive compendium on the Jameson clan published in 1901. She supplied a brief sketch of the early life of her father, Charles Jameson, an anecdote about her mother get-

ting lost in the woods for her father's entry,[24] and another longer
piece entitled "Memory Glimpses" for her own entry in the book.[25]
She later included all these pieces, with some expansions, in her
memoir. Perhaps recalling happier days in her long-ago childhood
provided a much-needed creative outlet during trying times.

In 1901 three of her sons – Joel, Will, and Charlie – obtained
homestead land for themselves and Sarah in Rouleau, a small settlement about seventy kilometres southwest of Regina in what was
then the Assiniboia District of the North-West Territories (now
Saskatchewan). Rouleau (famous today as the filming location for
the television comedy series *Corner Gas*) is still a very small town
with a population of only about five hundred, but in 1901 it was
inhabited by less than a hundred settlers.[26] That situation was
about to change, with the influx of many homesteaders from
Ontario and the United States.[27] Rouleau grew rapidly after the
Craigs arrived; it was incorporated as a village in 1903 and then as
a town in 1907, and became "the railway center of trade for the
whole area."[28] A description printed in the *Rouleau Enterprise* for
26 July 1905 praises the area's rich soil as ideal for growing wheat
and predicts a bright future for the community.[29] Fortunately, the
Craigs' timing was perfect for once: they were part of the first influx of settlers from Ontario who were able to get free homestead
land, while by about 1903 – only two years later – "little land was
left except by purchase from the CPR."[30]

While their older brothers were starting out on their new
properties, Lucy and Esther went to work in Illinois, where girls'
wages were better, in order to save and send home all they could
to contribute to the homestead cause. Finally, in August 1902,
Sarah's family – all except Albert and Frank – were on a train
bound for Rouleau. Thirty-eight years after she and Joel had

dreamed of taking up "homestead land in the great West" of the United States and planting their "Colony of Reformers," she was leading a much smaller but more congenial band of settlers to the Canadian west, to begin farming in earnest and finally earn a living at it if possible. This scheme at least held out the possibility of their gaining ownership of their own land.

It is interesting that the few family photographs that survive from this period, including one of Sarah and her children in Ontario, show none of the female family members – including Sarah – wearing the reform dress. As her diaries are completely silent during this period, there is no information on when or why the transition to normal clothing had occurred, and when she takes up her pen again after the move to the prairies, there is similarly no mention of the dress issue. Like the photograph taken in Ontario, those taken in Saskatchewan show Sarah in a long dress. However, Florence's account of the move from New Jersey to Ontario includes one tantalizing reference: she mentions that while Sarah and the girls were staying with Edwin and his family in Buffalo, another of Sarah's brothers, William, visited and gave her $5.00 to "buy a new dress." Apparently Edwin took her shopping at a ladies' wear store, where "she bought a very nice skirt and jacket suit in a light tan color, to be worn with a white blouse" (Memoir, part 2, 43–4). As a ready-to-wear garment, this skirt could not have been made in the reform style, but there is no mention of Sarah shortening it herself.

In an article entitled "Hygiene, Dress and Dress Reform," published in 1910, Dr Dudley Sargent lamented that, while "some evils" had been eradicated from women's dress, there was still work to be done in reforming fashion.[31] Nevertheless, it seems that numerous changes, including the move away from voluminous skirts and the shortening of hemlines, had made the reform dress obsolete, or at least not worth fighting for. The rise in the 1890s of bicycling costumes for women that were "bifurcated" for ease of movement provided a new vision of healthy female clothing;[32] similar garments were promoted by the Battle Creek Sanitarium.[33] And an alternative dress-reform movement, promoting "Artistic Dress" inspired by the loose, flowing garments of classical Greek statuary, was also having an influence.[34] Sarah does not mention any of these innovations in women's clothing in her diaries or memoir. Perhaps more pertinent, her diary accounts of her life on the prairies lack the evangelical fire that marked her earlier ones; she is no longer fighting for a cause, but instead simply searching for that road forward to a better life. Perhaps taking up the home-steading life at the age of sixty-two required energy enough and left little time to spend on crusading for the reform of women's fashions.

The family arrived on the prairie to face very primitive condi-tions. The area around Rouleau is very flat and extremely hot in the summer. The older boys had built shacks to house themselves, but the accommodations were basic. Sarah's first diary entry, for 16 August 1902, after they arrived in the dark and slept overnight in a field, describes her initial impressions:

After camping beside a haystack we rose in the early glory of the morning, saw the sunrise on the prairie, and spent some little time in contemplation of the grandeur and beauty of the scene ... Then packing our beds, we pushed on to Will's shanty (passing Rouleau by the way,) and arriving about 8:30. Took our breakfast and began to get acquainted with our surroundings The shanty was 12 x 12, with shed roof and

prairie soil for floor covered with the last years growth of
grass for a carpet; two small windows, a bed in one corner,
old box cupboard in another, a pile of "hop" in a third, and a
small short iron camp stone near the door. Some boards fas-
tened together and to the wall for a table complete the furniture. Rough and romantic enough, and here we women are
to stay while the boys put up the shell of a house on my claim
some 7 miles north and east of here. Rouleau, a little group
of buildings – schoolhouse, store or two, lumber yards, im-
plement shop, R.R. [railroad] siding and platform and some
dwellings – is about a mile-and-a half to the North. Boys
went to creek and brought up two barrels of water, as the
sloughs are about dry here. (Later diaries)

Sarah had one homestead claim, and Joel, Will, and Charlie each
had their own. The girls – Lucy, Esther, and Florence – lived with
Sarah but helped out wherever needed, sometimes keeping house
for their brothers. Every homesteader got 160 acres of free land for
a registration fee of $10.00.[35] The land had to be farmed for three
years; at that point, the holder of the claim could apply for a
"patent" and receive a deed to the property. The owner could then
draw loans on it to finance the next year's crops. Sarah received
her patent in 1904.

Life on the prairie was soon revealed to be a constant challenge.
Sarah and the girls had been on their farm for only ten days when
their shack was threatened by a prairie fire that they could see
burning to the southeast. For most of the day the fire looked as if
it was a long way off, and so the family retired for the night. However, the wind soon rose and drove the fire toward the Craig shack,
and rapid, heroic intervention was called for. "The boys rose

quickly, dressed, and with wet sacks fought the flames from 10 p.m. till 2 a.m. and had about conquered, when a light rain falling helped finish their work" (Later diaries, 27 August 1902).

Sarah's sons worked hard those first few weeks, fetching lumber and supplies from Rouleau, and although their work was delayed by a heavy hailstorm at one point, by September they had built a basic house for their mother and sisters. Sarah and the girls were able to move in on 10 September, less than a month after arriving on their claim. The new house was not complete – the door was only "stuck in" without hinges, and the roof boarded over with no shingles – but Sarah at once began to make it more homelike and was at least able to bake "camp-bread," biscuit dough rolled very thin, cut in pieces, and cooked in a frying pan on a camp stove (Later diaries).

That first winter on the prairie brought a startling wonder – a mirage – which Sarah describes lovingly in a long entry dated 26 November 1902 and entitled "The Mirage: by Mrs Craig." Perhaps she intended it to be published as a separate piece; it is certainly one of her more carefully crafted compositions.

This morning gave us a wonderful and beautiful surprise, tho' we were somewhat prepared for it by previous exhibitions on a smaller scale. It was a clear, sparkling, frosty morning, perfectly calm and still; every grass-blade and everything else out doors was covered with deep fairy-like feathers and ferns of frost. Looking toward sunrise, the whole prairie seemed a sea of shining silver, studded with pearls and diamonds flashing and sparkling in the sunlight. Seeing from the window, just after sunrise, that a *mirage* was in order, we went outside to get a better view, and were startled to find

ourselves encircled with groups of houses, out-buildings,
stacks &c. seemingly within hail! It actually looked as if our
neighbors far and near had lifted their possessions bodily,
bro't them near and set them down around our claim, and
were waiting to bid us good morning! Many of the houses we
had not known of at all; others we knew to be two to five or
even seven miles distant.

One curious feature of the wonder was that the most distant of the buildings, if in the same radial line of vision, came
up as near as the nearest, and stood sociably beside them,
during the *spell* of the mirage, but were the first to tumble
and disappear when the spell was breaking. Several of the
groups looked like small villages where had been only blank
prairie before; and we almost expected the villagers to step
out and exchange courtesies. There were gardens and plowed
fields and roads where only grass was visible yesterday; on
the North we could see the distant W.M. Trail to Regina, and
even the spectre of Regina itself over 20 miles distant. Far
off hills looked near, distant creek-banks near and high,
then further, and the usually invisible horizon was lifted
till we seemed to stand in a great basin, the near landscape
condensed as it were, bringing far off objects close.
(Later diaries)

If the prairie brought such marvellous beauty, it could also
bring sudden and deadly wildfires, such as the one that roared
through their area in April 1903, when an "ocean of fire swept by,
dividing and leaving the house untouched, but singeing our hair
and Joel's whiskers, and leaving some deep blisters" on Sarah's ear
and Joel's face (Later diaries, 10 April 1903). There were also deadly

lightning storms and hail that could destroy a crop in minutes.
Sarah describes a particularly frightening episode in 1907 when
ball lightning came down the metal stovepipe and into the house
during a storm, starting a couple of small fires in the kitchen and
leaving them all feeling as if they had been thumped on the head.
Fortunately, no one was hurt. There were other disadvantages too:
although the prairie land yielded increasingly good crops, frosts
often came as late as June and as early as August, threatening the
vegetables that the Craigs all needed to survive through the winter. And great howling blizzards often swept down without warning, endangering humans and animals alike. Furthermore, despite
farming full-time all summer and raising some cattle, the boys
had to supplement their earnings by working during the winter
at carpentering or other such jobs.

There were benefits for the family, however. Prairie life was
enlivened by the hearty cooperation of neighbours far and near,
especially at harvest time, and the social occasions that these
inevitably entailed. Even from the moment of their arrival, the
Craigs were welcomed by neighbours, from whom they borrowed
or bought much-needed household goods or provisions. There
was much visiting back and forth, and when fire destroyed one
neighbour's house in April 1903, Sarah welcomed the family in
temporarily. Furthermore, Rouleau, although just a small village,
was on a rail line, and thus larger towns were accessible. In places
such as Wascana and Regina, Florence was able to get work in a
store or the post office or later (once she had earned her diploma
at business college) as a bookkeeper – jobs well suited to a young
woman of considerable intelligence but limited physical endurance.
On the other hand, Esther, who had never finished school, seemed
unable to find any employment other than housekeeping, some

of it very arduous: "Jan. 29th, 1905. I had a letter from Esther, in
which she speaks of her work being *too hard*; and really, as she
describes it, (carrying in water to fill barrels – carrying coal from
outdoors down cellar for furnace, &c) it is too hard: doing a man's
work – or horse work, some of it – for girl's wages. I wrote at once
for her to give notice to leave, and come home for a rest" (Later diaries). Undoubtedly, the memory of the damage that such strenuous labour had done to Alice years before influenced Sarah's
decision. It must have also been disheartening to realize that such
heavy housework was still one of the few types of employment
open to young women.

The railway provided other opportunities for the younger
members of the family as well. Both Esther and Florence were involved in the Salvation Army (a natural alliance, considering the
family's long-standing interest in the temperance cause) and went
back and forth to work with the Army in Wascana and Regina at
various times. It was through this association that the two girls
met their future husbands, both of them Englishmen involved
with the Salvation Army. Esther married Arthur Wigglesworth in
1906, and Florence wed Edgar Blenkarn two years later.

Although these new family ties brought much joy to Sarah,
they also brought sadness at "losing" her daughters:

> May 29th Joel took Florence to the station today. So they
> come and so they go! God be with them! The sweetest part
> of a mother's life is the dear comradeship of her daughters.
> They cannot realize, as they go from her to make homes
> of their own, or from time to time for other reasons, that
> mother is giving up the dearest pleasure and solace she has
> in life. She gives it up – is ever giving it up – *almost* willingly

4.2 Esther Craig's wedding near Rouleau, Saskatchewan, in 1906

and even gladly, (for what seems to be their good) till the giving is over; then she is often almost overwhelmed by her loss! Where are the compensations? (Later diaries)

This heartfelt entry highlights one of the problems with the prairie situation: each of the boys had his own homestead and his own small house, while the girls lived with Sarah on her claim. As she got older, the loneliness brought on by the departure of her daughters was heightened by the separation of these dwellings from each other. The neighbours were kind, friendly people, but their houses were not close by; the nearest was a mile away. Sarah was left feeling isolated – not, at this point, on account of her style of dress, but simply by virtue of her children growing up. She seems to have been particularly affected by the departure of Florence, her youngest, whom she often describes as a happy girl with a "sunny face." Florence also had a good singing voice and could play the organ to accompany the family singing, in a version of the old "Craig family sing-alongs" that had apparently long been the custom. Although Sarah sometimes expresses her frustration that Florence is "the slowest hand at housekeeping I ever knew" (Later diaries, 14 February 1915), she clearly shared a deep emotional bond with her. The cheerful and capable Lucy remained with Sarah, but after so many years spent living with a house full of children, the transition must have been difficult.

Her loneliness is highlighted in her account of the traumatic return of her son Frank. According to Florence (in her additions to Sarah's memoir), Frank and Mellie's two sons had died of tuberculosis as children, and Frank himself had been afflicted off and on with the same disease. In 1905 he and Mellie moved to California for the dry climate, which was considered beneficial for those with lung problems. However, by 1906 he was dying, and a flurry of letters went back and forth between California and Rouleau. At first Mellie asked for financial support, but then later Frank wrote inquiring if he could come north to die in the arms of his family. Sarah's diary entries reveal both her love for her son and her desperate longing for companionship: "July 12th. 1906. A letter from Frank himself came last evening ... He realizes that he is soon going on his long journey, and is 'setting his house in order' ... Then my son asks: Will I open my home and heart to receive his wife when she is a widow, as he has no home to leave her, and she would have no other good one. God bless her and him. Yes, gladly. I wrote today and told him so. Then I'll

have a daughter at home, to stay at last. But it will be at the expense of a dear son's life!"

At one point it seemed that Frank and Mellie's church community in California had offered to support the couple themselves,
and Sarah was deeply disappointed. But then came a surprise:

Oct. 20th. Last night, after we had all retired and I had been
asleep, I heard voices – a call and answer – then a light, and
Joel ran downstairs. I came to the stairs and asked what was
up, and Joel said, "It's Frank and Mellie, Lucy says!" I hurried
on my wrapper and came down to greet my son and his wife
from California! What a surprise! Will found a letter from
Frank to me in the Office yesterday p.m. saying to look out
for them as they were coming; asking us to meet them with
wraps last eve. Accordingly he and Lucy did meet them, with
our buggy (which was still there) and she drove them home.
Frank was very tired and O *so* thin! But I knew them at once.
We made them comfortable for the night; and are arranging
them a part of the front room as he is not well able to climb
stairs. He rested well however, and looks better today. (Later
diaries, 20 October 1906)

Frank did not recover, however; he died on 18 December. And although Mellie stayed on for a few months, she did not prove to be
the "daughter" that Sarah had hoped for. Mellie certainly seems
to have gotten on well with the family, but simple economic necessity pressed her to move on. In June 1907 she left to return to
New Jersey, citing the lack of work for single women like herself on
the Canadian prairie. So ended that chapter, and Sarah's hope of
more female companionship.

It was during these years that she appears to have resumed writing seriously and began what she came to call her "History," the memoir of her life that she would leave unfinished at her death. She also mentions sending her material, including a number of poems, out to various magazines:

> Feb. 24, 1908 ... some manuscripts "returned with regrets"
> from the Youth's Companion [an American children's maga-
> zine]. I am doing a good bit of writing now – preparing an
> autobiographical sketch, to be connected with a biography
> of my husband, this as a legacy to my family.
> March 29, 1908. At last one of my poems has been accepted:
> "The voices of the Silence" appeared in the last Witness.
> I am pleased of course, but I hoped to have my pen bring
> me some returns in money to help missionary work at least.
> (Later diaries)

Specifically, Sarah wished to be able to support an orphan child in India or in Turkey, where the first massacre of Armenians had left many children orphaned and destitute. For some years she managed to send a few extra dollars to India, where she sponsored a young boy at a mission school until he found work; thereafter she assisted a young orphan girl in Turkey.

As for the farming, it was certainly a more successful venture than it had been in Ontario. The Craigs grew both wheat and oats, as well as hay. By 1905 the crop yields were fairly good – some 3,200 bushels of oats, for example. But not every year was successful: 1907 proved difficult, as grain prices were low. By this point, Sarah's sons Will and Joel had already begun looking for greener pastures. Charlie had married, sold his claim near Rouleau, and purchased

4.3 Harvest on the prairie, Rouleau, Saskatchewan

a larger one further north at Lily Plain, where he moved after his marriage. So he was not looking for better opportunities at that point. However, a land agent in town was actively promoting the fruit-growing lands of British Columbia, which were just opening up, and in September 1907 Will decided to go west and scout out the possibilities. He returned with a glowing report of the geography, climate, and economic prospects of the Kelowna area. This convinced Sarah and the rest of her children that making another move would be advantageous. The milder climate in British Columbia was a major factor, but also the cultivation of fruit trees seemed less physically demanding than growing acres of wheat and barley, and more suited to a family that lacked strong men with much stamina for hard labour. By 1908 plans were moving full steam ahead, and several offers were being discussed.

June 10th 1908. Will came home yesterday, packed his trunk,
helped Joel move cook stove to kitchen, last evening; and this
morning is off to his new place in "The Far West," to build a
stable and prepare to make it a home, visit his cousin Emory
in Kootenay district, and do various things.
June 25th. Lucy and Florence ... bro't me letters – one from
Will, who has decided to take 15 acres of land (cheaper, but
as good quality instead of the 12 he agreed for); and recom-
mends us to buy a few acres adjoining on higher land for a
building site, garden, fruit or chicken farm. (Later diaries)

Ironically, the Craigs' crop in the last year they were in Rouleau
was the best yet, amounting to over 7,000 bushels of good-qual-
ity grain (Later diaries, 9 October 1909). Yet the labour required to
produce that grain, and the constant worry about destructive
storms, early frosts, and unpredictable rainfall and temperature,
made the British Columbia option all the more attractive. Sarah
had certainly come to appreciate the beauty of the prairie in all its
seasons, and she sometimes described its changing colours in her
diary: "And again the face of the landscape is changing: the stooks
that dotted the farms, like tents of an invading army, have vanished; giant straw stooks loom here and there, guarding the gran-
aries and bins, while the 'histy, stibble fields' gleam pale gold in
the Autumn sunshine!" (Later diaries, 6 October 1908). However,
the hope of better opportunities beckoned.

Esther's husband, Arthur Wigglesworth, had purchased land
adjacent to the Craigs', and in March 1909 he went out to British
Columbia to meet Will there and help with building a first house
for Sarah and the family. Esther and their baby followed a couple

of weeks later. Yet Sarah's land on the prairie had not yet sold. Finally, in August of 1909, they were in luck:

August 7th. Went to Rouleau again on business intent, and this time met with success. Saw Mr How... when How heard Mr Johnston's offer he advised us to take it. We went to see Mr J. and he agreed to make it right with Mr H. So we closed the deal. We take 10 acres of land he has near Will's place in B.C. @ $225, and we have use of it for 3 years; then if we wish to sell it he buys it back @250 per acre. He pays us $1500.00 cash now, as much more Nov. 1st and balance next spring, interest on notes 6%. We get for our land $25.50 per acre – the 50 cts being Mr. How's commission. (Later diaries)

When the deal was finally concluded, they wrapped up their business quickly:

Nov. 10th. Just before seven this morning, Joel started for Rouleau to take train for B.C. Lucy and William went to town with him. He has the season's business about finished up. Most of the grain is sold; ... the year's bills all paid, except a part of the boy's wages ... Joel takes funds with him, to start building at once, left some money with me for immediate use; then there is the remainder of the grain to be sold, when prices are right: 200 bushels wheat, and nearly 1000 of oats. I have also a note from Mr Johnston for nearly $900.00 on my land coming due April 15th with interest 6%. My ten acres paid for, and Deed coming. (Later diaries)

Sarah Craig was nearly seventy years old at this point, and yet she was still vigorous enough to contemplate another major move in search of a better life. With some regret, but with great hope for a brighter future in British Columbia, she and Lucy boarded the train to begin their journey in late February 1910.

Chapter Five

Eden at Last

The journey westward from the flat prairie of Rouleau through the Rocky Mountains to Kelowna was an awe-inspiring experience. Sarah wrote the following diary account of her journey, which took her across several dramatically different geographies:

March 1st. Reached Calgary in early morning, after which the land began to rise and "roll," growing more and more rolling and hilly, till we were among the foothills and then mountains – small, big, and bigger: mountains great and mountains grand, mountains round, square and oval, and of no shape at all. We had taken a berth in a "Tourist" car; and by 10 a.m. the car was nearly empty, so we could look from both sides, seeing the best as we passed. We saw several of the notables "Three sisters," "Tower of Babel," "Mt Edith" and many others. But after noon it grew squally, and flying snow obscured much of the view. Also, the train was delayed by snow on track which had to be "plowed" off while we waited. Up near the "Great Divide" the snow was piled immensely on everything: houses, barns, outbuildings, capped with two and three feet of snow; and for hours in the upper

regions, little was to be seen but deep, fantastic snow-
wreaths; for the falling and flying snow veiled the mountains
most of the time.

   We should have been in Sicamous by 9:15 pm, to spend
the night at the Hotel; but snow prevented. Soon after dark
the snow plow was needed again; and it was doubtful if we
would reach Sicamous in time for the morning train. Berths
were made up, and we retired. Sometimes the train thun-
dered on, then stood still for hours. We were thankful when
the porter roused us in the early dawn, saying we would
reach Sicamous in 45 minutes. We were soon ready, and at
S. left the train to wait at station for another. Spent the time
walking about for exercise and fresh air. (Our train had been
very warm.) Soon we were riding thro' a beautiful country
toward Okanagan Landing. Often, where the road was cut
thro' a mountain, the rock, for quite a distance, seemed so
near the window it could be touched with the hand. Then
we whirled thro' beautiful forests, or past picturesque small
farms & orchards, and pretty farm houses, or lovely villages.
On the left, most of the way, was a narrow lake at first open
then covered with ice and snow.

   At this time, the railway did not extend all the way to Kelowna,
so travellers had to take a boat for the last portion of the journey.
The Craigs boarded the large paddlewheeler SS *Aberdeen* for "a
delightful ride down the lovely lake." Once they had arrived, Sarah
wrote enthusiastically about her new surroundings:

   We are delighted with our new home: the grand mountains
   of varying height – over and among which the fleecy clouds

gambol in the sunlight, the noble trees, and the lovely
Okanagan smiling up at us from the South West, are so
refreshing to our eyes just from the monotonous sameness
of the prairie, and we are ever finding something new to
charm the mind and please the eye. The house – *our* house –
stands a little above the valley, up a rather steep rise of a
few rods, the upper part of the lot being nearly level; then
Arthur's lot is on the next rise and nearer the mountain.
We are high enough for a good view, without too much
climbing. And the mountains are round about our
Jerusalem. (Later diaries, 10 March 1910)

Sarah's use of the phrase "our Jerusalem" suggests that this new
home signified to her at least the partial fulfillment of her utopian
dream. Instead of a colony of congenial strangers, she was surrounded by family members whose homes were close by, and who
were all involved in the project of farming in a lush, fruitful place
surrounded by stunning natural beauty. To her this was the Promised Land, her earthly Eden.

It is worth noting that, unlike many of the American women
who wrote diary accounts of their westward migrations in the
1850s and 1860s, Sarah never looks back.[1] Nor does she express any
nostalgia for the homes she has left behind once she has arrived
in Rouleau or in the Okanagan. She certainly misses members of
her family, particularly her parents, who continued to live in St
Stephen until they died of extreme old age. She always mentions
receiving letters from them and from her siblings, and from Joel's
mother, "Grannie Craig," and it is clear that she and her children
kept up a lively correspondence with friends and family in New
Brunswick, New Jersey, Buffalo, and Ontario. But Sarah's gaze is

always directed forward, toward the future and the brighter prospects that it might provide her. She does not indulge in nostalgia for the places of her past – places that had continually brought her failure and disappointment.

Sarah and her family had arrived in the Okanagan at a time when these lands were just opening up to orchard cultivation. Although white settlers had been coming for decades (to a Catholic mission and as prospectors in the gold rush), the extension of the Canadian Pacific Railway through the area in the 1890s sped up development. So did the introduction of fruit farming. Cattle ranching had flourished for years, and some farmers cultivated wheat, but once the Okanagan Valley's fruit-growing potential became known, land promoters began singing the praises of the area's climate and soil conditions to potential buyers.[2] The Scottish aristocrat Lord Aberdeen, Canada's governor general in the 1890s, and his wife accelerated this process after they purchased fruit-growing land near Vernon. They were so pleased with the natural beauty and climate of the area that they actively sought to attract British settlers to come and establish fruit farms in the Okanagan.[3] The SS *Aberdeen*, the comfortable sternwheeler on which Sarah and her family travelled from Okanagan Landing to Kelowna, was named after Lord and Lady Aberdeen and had been transporting passengers across the lake since 1893. It was the first paddlewheeler to provide regular service up and down the lake, and its impact was enormous; finally, settlers could make their way to areas previously considered inaccessible, or at the very least difficult to reach.[4]

Rutland, a small settlement at the foot of Black Mountain about eight miles east of Kelowna, had first been bought up by an Australian couple, the Rutlands, who saw the benches of flat land there as promising sites for apple orchards. It was John Rutland who organized the building of the irrigation system, with its flumes and ditches, that made growing fruit possible on some of the driest benches, including the lands that the Craigs purchased.[5] Because Rutland was a few miles out of town, land prices there were cheaper than in Kelowna and were thus within the means of poorer settlers such as Sarah and her family.

Despite the recent influx of newcomers, many of whom were "educated, worldly, and looking to replicate a familiar lifestyle," the Okanagan still retained a whiff of the "frontier" that it had been in the very recent past.[6] Many of the new arrivals, especially those from Britain and Europe, were glad to leave behind the stuffy "social constraints" of their motherlands and try out new ways of living.[7] People were unwilling to wait for politicians to approve projects that needed building but went ahead and took action themselves; for example, the community came together to raise funds for and build Kelowna's first hospital while there was still a population of less than a thousand people in the town.[8] In such an environment, the Craigs, finally in possession of a little capital realized from the sale of their prairie farms, were able to work hard and build a life for themselves.

Sarah clearly found the Okanagan landscape enchanting, but this was not the only attraction of her new home. In her diary account she pays great attention to describing the house itself, the first dwelling place she had ever been able to decorate as she wished: "April 9th 1910. Such a week of cleaning! ... All done at last, most of the rooms re-oiled, kitchen floor painted, stove replaced; beds set up in bedrooms & three doors hung. Joel and I slept in our milk white rooms last night ... It is a beautiful home, and will grow in beauty and hominess as the plan is worked out to a finish.

It seems almost too good to be true that at last I – we – have a home place that we can beautify as we wish. Our Father is so very good to us!" It is worth noting that Joel, Will, and Lucy all shared the new house with their mother. Whatever these grown children thought of this arrangement, it most certainly ensured that Sarah was less lonely and that she was able to have help with the housework that she found increasingly challenging as she grew older. The presence of Esther and Arthur and their family just up the hill, and of Florence and Edgar next door for several years, made this situation as much like a "colony" as possible under the circumstances.

In June, Florence and Edgar travelled from Rouleau to join the family with their three-week-old baby boy, Freddie, and took up residence on land adjacent to Sarah's. The cluster of three family farms comprised many acres of land. One by one tents, shacks, and then more solid structures were built to house everyone, and improvements made as time went on. Christmas 1912 was a glad affair, enlivened by the family's new ability to afford a few gifts for each other and by the presence of Sarah's first grandchildren. Esther and Arthur's adopted son, Richard, and Florence and Edgar's first child, Freddie, lit up the family celebrations in the new home.

> December 25th. Richard and Freddie are the glad possessors of Christmas sleds this morning! How they run! Dinner time brings all old and young to Grandma's *where Christmas is supposed to be!* Dinner over and cleared away, Richard goes out with his sled, Freddie goes to bed; and quiet preparations are going forward in the attic. Between 6 and 7 we are called to the "Sky parlor" and ascend to a cosy room, with a stove

giving heat, rugs on the floor, a couch, baby carriage, arm-
chair for Grandma, and for centerpiece the Christmas tree
gleaming and sparkling with candles, tinsel and presents!
Arthur was deputed by Santa to distribute the gifts. Each little boy got an armful of pets – dolls, pussycats, teddy bears
and gorrillas, a white lion, &c, some new and several old and
dressed over (from a neighbor) and each has a musical top,
which gives them and their papas and uncles too great delight. (Later diaries)

The family immediately saw the advantages of the Okanagan
climate: they were able to sow vegetable seeds in late March and
have the plants developing by late April. They put in orchard trees
in the middle of April. This was all such a welcome change from
the prairies. Sarah threw herself into the farming work as much as
she was able, planting vegetables and picking fruit. Indeed, the
new home in British Columbia contained many delights for her.
While the diaries written during the prairie years in Rouleau do
include some descriptions of natural beauty, the number and
length of such descriptions expand dramatically during the BC
years. Sarah seems to have found in the scenery renewed inspiration for her literary skills, almost as if she had "met the Muse" all
over again. Life in Rutland seems to have involved frequent picnics
in the woods and excursions out of doors, occasions that she rel-
ished to the full, always describing them in loving detail. It is evident from her diary entries that she was walking and climbing
during these outings, not just sitting and observing from the side-
lines – quite remarkable activity considering that she was now almost seventy years old.

May 1, 1910. Sunday. All the two families except Will took a
ten mile drive over hill and dale, thro' parts of the country
new to us all ... Everywhere fine orchards coming into glorious bloom, alternating with fine gardens and fields of crop,
while cattle and horses pastured in the untilled lands between ... Up hill and down we went – mostly *up* – thro'
sweet pine forests, where fir and spruce were mixed in as
well, forests of poplar, and balm of Gilead, birch, maple, wild
cherry, and others, over ditches, creeks, and little babbling
rills; but mostly the way was thro' the fragrant orchards –
the glory of BC.

Sarah goes on to describe the kind of rigorous hike through
rough terrain and narrow trails that many people much younger
than she was would never have attempted:

May 22. After service, Will took us some miles farther, past
beautiful landscapes, then up, up winding trails and along
"benches," still up to the head of the O.L. [Okanagan Land-
ing] Co.'s ditch, where the icy cold water tumbles down
a three-story cascade between split rocks – perpendicular
crags, so high it almost made us giddy to look up at them
into the big flume ...We had left horse & buggy behind at
a shed, and toe-nailed it along a path hardly wide enough
for our feet, around a *steep* hillside, catching at tree trunks,
bushes, or tufts of grass to steady our steps (Will looking
sharp that I was safe) till we reached the dam, scrambled
down and over it and bathed our faces, rested and cooled off.

Such outings became cherished routines in the summertime,
and even as Sarah grew older, she still found great pleasure in her

hands-on approach to enjoying nature. Unconventional as always, she defied the expectations of how an older woman should behave in the outdoors in order to enjoy herself to the fullest:

July 4th, 1912. Sunday School picnic at Scotty creek. We all went and enjoyed a very pleasant outing, on a favourable day ... There were two swings, and a store of ice cream – our democrat [wagon] being utilized as a store. I ate more ice creame than ever in one day before – 5 cones. After dinner I had a swing! It took two women to *lift me in* (the swing was high) while Mr Vance held the rope steady. It was tho't surprising for so old a lady to join in such youthful sports. Later, I took a quilt and went apart from the merry groups of old and young to a quiet spot under the trees, spread my couch & laid me down to rest. Looking up thro' the green leafy boughs with the flowing water murmuring in my ear, I soon fell asleep; had a good refreshing nap and lay for sometime after waking before I cared to rise. Then bathing my face and combing my hair, I rejoined the party, some of whom tho't it strange for anyone to lie down in the woods where bugs and beetles might crawl over one; but it was delightful!

In this description, Sarah seems completely at one with her environment. The shade, the hypnotic sound of the water, and the soft forest floor combine with the dreamland of sleep to hold her gently in a quiet paradise. These same woodlands appear again and again in her diaries.

July 1, 1914. Shady woods, rippling water, singing birds, with the merry voices and laughter of picnicers blended in a harmonious whole. After dinner ... many of us went to the lake

shore, watched the boats, paddled our feet in the water
&c … Later, I had a ride on the lake with some girls.
July 4, 1917. Two Sunday Schools and everybody else so in-
clined, convened in a favorable spot beside Mission Creek,
for a Dominion Day picnic … The lovely weather, the tall
trees, so beautiful in the glistening green of their leafy
dresses, tossing their branches in the fresh, cool breezes;
the towering, precipitous mountain-sides & the rippling,
flashing babbling stream at its foot – each and all combined,
with social, kindly human life at its best, and abundance of
good, appetizing eatables.

Summer was not the only season when such outings occurred,
and Sarah made a point of recounting in detail an autumn hike in
the forest:

Oct. 15, 1916. I have been longing for an outing. So after
Sunday School I proposed that we take the "Wiggs" [Wig-
glesworths] and go for a drive along some of the mountain
roads, leading thro' autumn woods … And what a delightful
drive we had! First past the settlement, up into the piney
ridges, some distance; then to the right, along the mountain
sides, overlooking stretches of deciduous forest, strips, belts,
slumps, lining the valley below us all gorgeously dressed in
flaming Autumn hues – green & gold, but mostly gold, with
touches & splashes of scarlet sumach, & other variations.
O! It was grand – glorious! … This is the first outing in the
Autumn woods I have had in BC & Esther said the same; we
have passed by them on the road; but today we went *thro'*
them – *under* them – watched the lowering sun shine thro'

5.1 Picnic in the woods near Rutland, British Columbia

the golden leaves; stopped the horse & got down and
tramped thro the rustling fallen leaves, gathered branches
to bring home, &c.

Here again Sarah is unwilling to be merely a spectator; she wants
to walk among those rustling leaves herself and enjoy the moment
with all of her senses.

She never explicitly says so, but the Okanagan landscape
may have reminded her of the forests, rivers, and mountains of
New Brunswick, through which she had rambled happily in her
youth, and which she had lovingly described in a piece called the

"Blueberrying Story," perhaps intended for publication, that she incorporated into her memoir (18–20). If so, these mountains were higher and even more beautiful than those she had left behind. Unlike many women settlers who came west, Sarah had not left a "civilized" urban environment with all the amenities of late nineteenth-century life, but a series of difficult rural and semi-rural situations. Thus she can write about this lush forest with clear-eyed appreciation untainted by nostalgia for a longed-for homeland; she certainly has no interest in "civilizing" this wild landscape, as many female settlers did.[9] Her deep emotional connection with this environment is clear. In accepting it as her "Eden," she cherishes it both for what it represents to her and for what it *is*: its beautiful, untamed self.

As the years rolled on, Sarah wrote in her diary of the increasing improvements to her house: a picture rail to enable her to put up photos of her loved ones, the installation of a real bathroom, the painting of the walls in lovely colours that made her room look "very dainty and pretty" (Later diaries, 27 November 1918). Although the indoor plumbing, added in 1919, was surely a greatly appreciated convenience, it is the aesthetic improvements, the details that make her living spaces more beautiful, that she tends to dwell on in her diary descriptions. "Dec. 23, 1918. The boys moved the furniture & laid the carpet this p.m. It was a difficult – or rather a painstaking job, and took them all the daylight after dinner & an hour or two of lamplight. But it brightens the room wonderfully! The light color, green leaves and dark red flowers are such a cheery contrast to the old, worn, darkened paint we have been looking at so long! I cut & partly made new curtains for parlor window of pretty, rose-bordered scrim." The colours she chooses are invariably those of nature – the greens of leaves, the rich hues of flowers – as if she is intent on bringing into her rooms the vitality and sweetness of the world outside that she loves so much.

Fruit farming in British Columbia was truly a cooperative venture for the family, and since their lands were adjacent to one another, the Craigs all helped with the picking and whatever else needed to be done. Sarah willingly did as much as she could, despite the weakness that came with increasing age. The amount of physical labour that she was still able to manage, even in her late seventies, is amazing; she often mentions climbing the apple trees to pick the fruit on the middle branches. "Sept 14, 1918. Will took a load of apples to town yesterday: & has the rack loaded up with mine now, going down to the barn for an early start Monday. I picked about 25 boxes today; besides what I had done the other days. Lucy did 30 yesterday. O it is delightful work! And tho' it tires me it is food for me." She seems to have taken special pleasure in sitting up in the trees close to the fruit.

As the orchard trees matured, the crops became more bountiful, and Sarah expresses both thankfulness and pleasure at having money to spend. After a lifetime of deprivation, she is particularly eager to spend money on books of all sorts, both the classics and the latest Canadian bestsellers, recording in her diary:

Dec. 8th 1915. The joy and beauty of having money is in spending it where it will do good! Praise the Lord. I can put the most of mine to good & much needed use. Gave Lucy $10.00, paid Will my water tax – $25.00; set apart other sums, and sent a few dollars to Eaton for Christmas goods to make the little ones glad and a few bits for myself.

Dec. 14th. I made out an order tonight for a few books – 9 volumes – from William Briggs Toronto.

19th. This morning (Sunday) while at my bath, Lucy called to
me, did I know my express had come: it was our Christmas
things from Eaton's – several presents for both mamas and
children, and in my share some things for myself. One, a
beautiful copy of William Wordsworth's poems, which will
be a pleasure to me for many years if I am here so long.
June 17th. 1917 I received another most acceptable birthday
gift last night – a beautiful story from the delightful pen of
"Ralph Connor," inscribed "To my mother, in honor of her
77th Birthday: with love from Esther."

By 1917 the fruit farming was becoming quite profitable as a result of greater yields from their maturing trees and the higher
prices paid for fruit during the war.

Oct. 10th 1918. Will took a load of fruit in for Esther today;
and bro't us cheques for all fruit delivered *before* (except
previously paid for) mine being for $367.77 & Esther's over
$500.00. He got his own cheque and cashed it.
Oct. 11. Esther & I sent our cheques today to be cashed, & the
bulk of amounts left in bank. How often I have longed for
money (as who has not?) to handle freely! Not at all alone
for my own & family's use, but to be able to *give* – to *give* to
needy causes & persons. Thanks to my Father I now have
the privilege of *giving* on a small scale, at least!
Oct. 19, 1918. A bounteous year it has been to this ranch &
others, like this & Esther's, that were too high for the spring
frost. But it is the exceedingly high prices of fruit that fill our
purses; for *my* crop was not as large as last year: Esther's
much larger; her trees having only started bearing last year.
(Later diaries)

After so many decades of penny-pinching and having barely enough to feed her family, Sarah seems especially glad to celebrate Christmas with gift giving. Each year her diary entries describe in loving detail the preparations made and the presents exchanged.

Dec. 25, 1915. The time-honored holiday, and a house full of guests. Having retired late last night, we did not rise early. Freddie & I were first on deck; he to see if "Santa" had filled his stocking, and I to look for fire to start *my* fire. I found plenty; and he found a kit of boys tools beside his stocking, which had something in it also. We went back & dressed. Fannie came down and soon both were happy with their stockings, and Freddie with hammer and saw was doing a stunt on the kindling wood. Three men went to morning service; Lucy put up and trimmed the tree (J.B. & Mr Mugford got trees and cedar boughs for the church & our 2 houses on Thursday) and hung cedar & holly. After dinner the "Wiggs" came down and spent the evening. After some music, the presents were bro't out, and each found one to several articles bearing their name.

The growing number of grandchildren was a source of great happiness, although as Sarah grew older, caring for the little ones required more effort. This was particularly evident when three of Florence's five children came down with chicken pox one after another in 1918. They all came to stay with Sarah in Rutland, and at times she was left to look after the baby, Alice Beatrice, all on her own. Nevertheless, when the sickness had passed and Florence took them all home, she wrote that the house was "painfully silent" and she missed "the busy hum, the prattle, the rattle of feet, racing to & fro, the slamming of doors, and all the noise, buzz & hustle that five rollicking children can make!" (Later diaries, 16 August 1918).

Sarah's appreciation of the natural beauty of her own property is another constant theme. From the beginning, her diaries are full of loving descriptions of the new land: "June 22nd. 1913. O! The delicious scent of the clover as the wind wafts it up from the orchard! It is good to see a field of timothy and clover on my own land again; and the cows enjoy their feed of juicy green hay morning and night too. My garden is filling with flowers, but the little edging of white clover in front of it is one of its chief beauties in my eye. The big 'Buckeye Briar' rose I bro't from the prairie (a scion of those we had in N.B. sent me by Mrs. Stewart) has bloomed long and profusely this season."

Sarah was particularly fond of her upper bedroom, which she called her "Sky Parlor" for its magnificent view of the valley and lake. She used this as a summer bedroom, moving downstairs in the winter for greater warmth and to spare her aging legs from having to climb stairs in the cold weather. But it is clear that she derived keen pleasure from looking out the room's window with its panoramic view of the valley. In 1917 she writes, "I can't give up my nice summer chamber, over-looking the beautiful valley – not till *I must!* I will enjoy it this summer at least; and try to have my winter room beautified a bit before cold weather."

Gardening also became something of an obsession for Sarah. In her earlier writings, she always mentions beautiful flowers, and she had clearly tried her best to grow what she could in Rouleau, even if it meant forcing bulbs indoors; but the climate in British Columbia was much more conducive to growing things and in greater variety. "Aug. 10th 1914. O how much I am enjoying my great, beautiful lily, which has been in bloom several days; the

5.2 Sarah Craig's house in Rutland, British Columbia

Japan golden band and 'lilium auratum,' which I have wanted so
long. 5 great flowers now open; some will soon fall; but tiger lilies
are coming on and another – a 'Speciosum.' Aster blooms are fast
filling up the garden and 2 great clumps of white phlox make an
immense mass of snowy beauty! Am watering them today" (Later
diaries).

Bulbs and seeds were by this time available through mail-order
companies, and Sarah spent many hours poring over nursery

catalogues as soon as they arrived in the winter. She developed "almost a mania – an obsession" for flowers, writing one March, when the weather was still too cool to plant anything, "I eat and drink and sleep and dream flowers!" (Later diaries, 15 March 1914). She could never afford to order all the items she wished for, but she did know how to propagate new plants from cuttings and roots, and her thrifty choices eventually paid off. In only a few years her patient nurturing of cuttings had resulted in a beautiful garden with flowering vines trailing along the front of her porch. One diary entry reads: "Aug. 30, 1914. Another bright and glorious day, but quite cool, like a forerunner of Autumn. All the air full of perfume of flowers, and music of birds and bees; I can *see* the musicians, and imagine their music. The vine-covered porch is a bower of perfume, two stories high."

During these years Sarah continued to work on her memoir, and she mentions it often in her diary entries for Sundays. She seems to have interspersed reading books with writing the memoir, a process that undoubtedly contributed to its literary qualities. She is noticeably more conscious as the years roll on that she might not live to finish it: "Aug. 25th. 1918. Besides my usual reading & studies, having no letters awaiting answers, I bro't out my History, and wrote several pages. Seems good to be at it again – living over the happenings, doings & special Providences of the past. I must try to keep it going on toward a finish, lest night overtake me ere my work is done!"

She was also clearly continuing to submit items for publication, and finally these efforts began to bring some success:

Dec. 13th, 1913. When J. came home tonight he bro't me a letter from Miss Sangster of C.H. [*Christian Herald*] accepting a little poem I sent, and promising me a cheque when it is printed! It will be my *first* pay from paper or magazine for a poetry or prose article, tho' many of both have been published.

July 13, 1916. Wrote a few remarks to read before the meeting, re "Home Buying," which is so strongly urged upon us at present. I stated the fact that BC Products were sold for less in Regina, Winnipeg, & other far off eastern places than here; proposing that we look into the matter or lay it before the editors of the Consumers' Magazine. My remarks were not only approved, but at once nabbed for publication!

British Columbia also provided new social opportunities for Sarah's children. Lucy and Will went to literary society meetings and political lectures, Will and Joel joined the fruit growers' association, and Lucy was heavily involved in the Ladies Aid Society as well as the church. She is depicted in the diary accounts as the most adventurous of the girls – going skating every winter, climbing mountains, joining the men in fishing expeditions, and generally seeming more active than other young women of her time. For instance, during an account of a Dominion Day picnic in 1915, Sarah mentions Lucy's swim in an old dress, and she is always the hiker who climbs to the top of a ridge to look over a dizzying drop. Lucy must have reminded Sarah of her own unconventional younger self.

Sarah herself seems to have loosened up in her last years. The frontier atmosphere in Kelowna in those days may have encouraged this evolution, since from the beginning the area had been settled by those looking for adventure and opportunity. Despite her advancing age, Sarah seems to have taken every opportunity

5.3 Lucy Craig picking fruit, Rutland, British Columbia

to enjoy new experiences. In 1915, when she was seventy-five, the chance of a lifetime came her way when four of her brothers – Edwin, Henry, Howard, and William Jameson – made a trip west to visit her in British Columbia and then took her with them down the coast to Brinnon, Washington, to visit their eldest brother, Isaac. He was by then a depressed widower, his wife of many years,

Jemima, having recently died. Sarah describes their trip in vivid detail in her diary: sailing down Okanagan Lake to take the train to Vancouver, from there to Victoria and across to Washington, and through Seattle and south to Brinnon, a very small forest settlement where Isaac had built a fairly primitive house.

Aug. 8, 1915. Left the rig at old camp and walked some 40 rods farther up; part of the way being so narrow, rough & steep – over logs, stones, tree-roots &c, it took two men to get me over it safely. But we had our reward in a sublime view of a glorious waterfall: way up, up, near the clouds it seemed, it tumbled into view, a sheet of snowy foam, rushing headlong down the rocky gorge. Perhaps halfway down the rock bellied outward, like a hoop petticoat, breaking the stream into many small streams, which raced down the skirt folds to bottom, or broke and started anew. *And Edwin had forgotten his Kodak!*

Isaac decided to travel back to British Columbia with his sister and visit with her and her family, and so the reunion was prolonged. After the other brothers went on to visit other friends on the west coast, Isaac travelled back to Rutland with Sarah. He enjoyed himself hugely, and it was as if the beauty of this landscape breathed some life back into him:

Sept. 5th. 1915. After Sunday School, and dinner, Isaac, myself & Lucy, with Will as driver, took a ride thro' and around part of the valley South west of home, also climbing certain altitudes by way of following the road, and getting good viewpoints. Just two weeks ago the same hours (or one of them)

5.4 Sarah and her brothers in 1915

he & I, with the Johnstons were whirling thro' orchards &
parks near Vernon, today, we showed him still more of the
beauties of BC – the K.L.O. [Kelowna Lake Okanagan] lands
and orchards, &c with wood, creek and mountain thrown in.
He enjoyed it very much; is highly impressed in favor of our
country. (Later diaries)

Isaac prolonged his stay in Rutland with Sarah and her family by
several weeks, leaving only reluctantly. Unfortunately, the health

benefits he seems to have enjoyed in British Columbia dissipated once he returned home to Brinnon, probably at least partly because of his solitary life there in the woods. Apparently, his son George was with him only part of the year, and the rest of the time he was alone, trying to manage by himself at the age of seventy-nine. The following year Sarah received a letter from him in which he expressed a desire to return to Rutland and live out his remaining days with her and her family; "I wrote him today that we would all be glad to have him come & anchor here with us" (Later diaries, 28 August 1917). However, Isaac never did make the journey and he died that October.

As was the case for many, Sarah's last years were deeply affected by World War I. The most immediate effect was an increase in prices for every kind of foodstuff. She writes in her diary: "Aug. 5th, 1914. War between England & Germany, of which we have heard rumors for some days, seems now to be a fixed fact; and prices of provisions &c. are soaring accordingly. Everybody is in a hurry to lay in a stock of flour, sugar, and other stuff before prices go higher." The social networks she had begun building as soon as she arrived – at the two churches she attended (in Rutland and Kelowna) and her Ladies Aid Society – became more active with the advent of war. The Ladies Aid Society held socials and apron sales to raise funds for the Red Cross and the Canadian Patriotic Fund, and everyone was involved in knitting warm mittens and socks and in baking and packing boxes of supplies for the soldiers overseas.

The community also mounted entertainments that supported the war effort; for instance, in December 1914 Sarah and her family attended a performance of a patriotic play at the schoolhouse. She describes it as follows:

December 1st· Thirteen ladies dressing in purest white, with
red sashes, sang the "Red, White and Blue," which was followed by a number of Patriotic Songs; (some comic, but
mostly serious) ... But the chief attraction was the climax,
when the curtain was drawn aside, showing the soldiers, just
from the trenches, sitting or lounging around their camp fire,
talking, reading, singing – two or three smoking – warming
hands or feet over the sham fire, which looked *very* natural;
while a crescent moon hung overhead & the pines forming
a background for the scene, frequently shaken by the wind –
or some other force. A forlorn, delapidated looking group, in
more or less ragged garments of faded khaki, or similar
color; weary, yet making brave efforts to rally each other's
spirits, with fife, mouth organ, and camp songs like Annie
Laurie and others. (Later diaries)

The performance ended with everyone singing "God Save the
King" and was "vigorously applauded."

As always, Sarah was intent on keeping herself informed about
larger world events. When both her sons-in-law, Arthur and Edgar,
and then her son Charlie enlisted, these efforts became more personal. She had been supporting orphan children for some years,
sending much of her spare cash overseas. Now she did what work
she could to support the soldiers. But she did not let patriotism
cloud her view of the horrors of war: "Nov. 28, 1914. Another week
has passed into history – spent by us in quiet, peaceful ways; but
Oh, how different it has been to the many thousands involved in
war, terrible, unspeakable war! Not only those suffering untold
hardships & their death in the fighting line, but those at home –
their families, whose breadwinners were snatched from them to

kill other breadwinners of other wives and children! Alas! Alas! How long, oh Lord! How long?" (Later diaries).

In fact, although patriotism played some role in their decisions, Edgar and Charlie seem to have joined up as soldiers mainly for the steady wages that military service provided. By this time, Charlie's marriage had fallen apart and he had moved to British Columbia to join his family; restless and in need of income, he hoped that employment in the army would provide new opportunities. Edgar, although never in good health, now had five young children to provide for, and his training as a journalist brought him only sporadic employment in Kelowna. The promise of a steady income was a powerful inducement. He joined the Rocky Mountain Rangers in 1916 and was sent overseas the following year to serve in Belgium and France.

One of the great tragedies of these last years of Sarah's life was the death of Esther's husband, Arthur, in action. The family had earlier received word that a bullet had passed through his pocket, flying in one side and out the other and leaving him miraculously unharmed. He had also been one of only two survivors of a fierce battle. Sarah's account in her diary of the tragic news that he had been killed juxtaposes an idyllic scene of women picking fruit in an Edenic setting with the brutal reality of his death:

Sept. 17, 1917. I picked the low fruit on one tree then climbed into the crotch of the tree, and worked among the limbs. Esther came with Doris & Alfred and we were working away happily, when Lucy came over, with the sudden and awful news that Arthur – our Arthur has been "killed in action!" Like a "bolt from the blue" came the tidings, overwhelming us all for the time in a tidal wave of bewildering grief! The dear boy has seemed almost to bear a "charmed life" for so long – has been thro' some of the fiercest fighting and roughest scenes of the war, without a scratch before – that we dared to hope it might continue! And now to be told we shall never see his bright merry face, or hear his cheery whistle again! – how *can* we realize it?

Esther, now widowed with several small children to care for, was of course shattered, and Sarah and her other daughters had to rally round to help her. Meanwhile, Edgar, never physically strong, was "invalided for shell shock" (what we now call post-traumatic stress disorder) and spent the rest of the war in hospitals and military bases in England. Sarah's diary entry for 11 November 1918 reflects the joy and relief everyone felt at the news that Germany had surrendered and the war was over. All the whistles and horns in Kelowna were sounding to signal the joyful news: "11th. *Peace! Peace!! peace!!!* Sweet peace at last! Between 9 & 10 a.m. hearing the Kelowna whistles blowing 'like mad' J.B. called 'Central' to ask what it was. 'Can't hear anything for the blamed whistles!' came the answer, 'but it's peace!'"

The war had brought a few compensations as well as new attitudes and opportunities for women. With many of the men overseas, even those women who were not widows were left at home tending the farms and found themselves with unanticipated freedoms. It is at this point, near the very end of her life, that Sarah returns to the reform-dress theme, encouraged not by the upper-class women of New Jersey or Boston but by the ordinary farm women for whom the reform dress had always held the greatest appeal. The sight of her friend and neighbour Mrs Gray prompts her to write in her diary:

July 18th. 1917. This morning, behold! Mrs Gray came danc-
ing in, in a pair of her absent boy's pants & a white blouse,
looking nice & cool for her irrigating work. Reminded me
of my years pioneering the American Costume.
21st. Mrs. G called (for her milk) just in a pair of *ladies' overalls* with bib, & gathered at ankles. Good! I'll make some!

In later entries she records:

Oct. 6th. I finished my outdoor suit today – loose wide
trousers and blouse – and it is very neat & trim. When I have
altered the suit I bought, I will be outfitted for picking fruit
&c. And I have several tons yet to pick.
Aug 9th 1918. Donned my overall suit and picked plums, with
J. B. Will picked crabs and prunes. I picked all the ripe fruit I
could reach & quit.

Unfortunately, no photographs survive of Sarah in her overalls.
    Of course, times were changing for all women, and among
these advances was at last gaining the right to vote: "May 7th 1917.
Esther and I went to Post-office toward evening; returning, called
at Registrar Scofield's office and entered our names as VOTERS!
So I have lived to see the cause won, for which I helped to do
battle in my young days! Praise the God of Righteousness." It is
not clear whether she refers here to any direct involvement in the
suffragette movement; if she did take an active part, she never
mentions it in her surviving diaries. She may simply be referring
to her lifelong fight for women's equality, a cause embodied for
her in the dress-reform and water-cure movements and in the
colony scheme that she dreamed of for so many years. Her

strongest female role models in the reform movements, such as
Harriet Austin, Ellen Beard Harman and Mary Tillotson, were all
deeply involved in the ongoing campaign for women's rights. Ironically, Canadian women got the vote federally in 1918, two years
before American women did.

Sarah appears to have retained her allegiance to simple water-
cure methods of home doctoring even while accepting the need
for professional help in more serious cases, such as when she broke
her right wrist in January 1912. Her diary entries concerning that
incident – written soon after, in awkward, large writing – indicate
that she went straight to the hospital and had the fracture set and
dressed. However, she still deemed other ailments treatable by
water-cure methods, and she resisted the newer medical treatments prescribed by doctors. "Dec. 10th 1918. Dr Knox ... came
this morning to see Esther: pronounced her ailment 'bronchitis';
left medication & directions for treatment, diet, &c. Does not
think her case dangerous; but it might become so. Bade her go to
bed and stay there till better. So she went. I wouldn't use his *blisters* (hot fomentations are better) but Lucy is Nurse in charge, and
has little faith in her mother's simple medical methods, which suf-
ficed to raise a large family successfully, & without doctors' bills!"
This last statement is, of course, a bit disingenuous: although her
methods succeeded in many cases, she lost two young children
and her beloved Alice to illnesses that could not be successfully
treated by water-cure methods.

Sarah had been suffering increasing deafness over the years and
had long had trouble hearing what went on in church; only some
preachers spoke clearly enough that she could hear their sermons.
She had tried numerous remedies, including a mail-order hear-

ing aid, a set of "Morley Phones," which proved ineffectual, and her hearing had only become worse. It reached the point where she could not hear much of the social conversation around her. To compensate for this loss, her diaries suggest, she occasionally indulged in jokes and pranks near the end of her life.

> March 28th 1918. A party of some 40 at least were gathered, and made the time pass happily, with music, games, and friendly discourse. Two girls bro't in Mrs. Shell's twins – 3 months old – which were greeted with shouts of gleeful applause. Then I took a tho't to have a bit of fun (I was just sitting "Mum" most of the time); so I stepped forward saying "These babies are mine: I want them" and taking one on each arm, I walked into the Parlor among the gentlemen offering to give them away while the mother and all the crowd were convulsed with laughter. No one offered to take the wee dears till I reached Mr Flemming on the far side of the room & deposited them in his willing arms (more shouts of laughter!) turned & walked away, amid great merriment all round. After a few minutes, however, I went and rescued the babies, restored them to their mother and took my seat, feeling that *I* had a share in the jollification on my own hook.

Sarah seems to have mellowed in other ways as well. While her reactions in earlier days to issues such as her sister's abandonment of the reform dress were extreme and reflected a very polarized world view, by the time she moved to Rutland she was able to adopt a more nuanced approach to complex questions, even those about which she had strong opinions, such as temperance. This

evolution is vividly illustrated in her advice to her former daugh-
ter-in-law Mellie, who left Rouleau a few months after Frank's
death to return to New Jersey, her original home. Mellie had met
Frank when both were involved in the Salvation Army, and so her
views on alcohol were undoubtedly strict. In 1912 she remarried,
but the marriage got off to a rocky start, according to Sarah's diaries. "Nov. 1, 1912. A letter from Mellie tonight announces that
she was to be wedded yesterday! To a widower blacksmith who
had been living alone for nearly five years. I am very, very glad for
her, to think she has a home of her own, instead of sewing like a
slave in the factories and making little more than expenses. I hope
she has found a *good* man who will be a good husband. God bless
them both."

However, the couple had not been married long before there
was trouble.

Apr. 20, 1913. I have neglected to tell you, my Diary, about the
last change in Mellie's life. Soon after Christmas – just after
her Christmas letter, telling of their dinner, presents, company &c., came a note saying we might write to her old address till further news, which we did. After weeks of waiting,
came a letter from her new home, but no explanation. However, the *next* letter told us that one day when they were in
town, he *took a drink of liquor*! which he had vowed not to
do, and the next day she packed and left. But he begged so,
she went back vowing that the *next* time she would *stay* left.
Sure enough the next time came (lately) he got really drunk
& she went and *stayed* ...

I wrote Mellie last week, saying how sorry I felt for them both, suggesting, and half advising that, as a man of his age, who never drank but *occasionally*, will not become a drunkard (unless out of pure grief at losing her), that now since she has made her word good, she might forgive him and make him and herself happy again by helping him be the man he wants to be. I don't know what she will think of it. But I wish they could be happily reunited.

Such an attitude of compromise is astonishing in light of Sarah's earlier rigid views. But a lifetime of experience seems finally to have mellowed her and given her wisdom. And it would seem that Mellie took Sarah's advice, since her next letter, in October 1913, indicated that she and her husband were back together: "Oct. 23rd. Mellie writes that her husband invites me to go and spend the winter months with them! If money was *plenty* I might go help them eat their Christmas turkey. She sent me a geranium slip. It came today and I potted it." This is the last diary entry about Mellie, but it suggests that she and her husband appreciated Sarah's advice and wished to communicate their gratitude.

Sarah's diaries break off about three weeks before her death. Esther and Lucy had gone away to the west coast for a much-needed vacation, and although Sarah did receive some assistance with the housework, it seems that no full-time housekeeping help was available to her, and she succumbed to the strain. Her last letter to Florence expresses exhaustion but also an unwillingness to call her daughters home. She writes, "The girls' trip, which I was as glad of as they, has keeled me over in the worst way … I do a little bit; but I am *so* week! I was so week some days I *couldn't breathe right* – just little short catchy puffs several times ... the girls do not know, yet, how I went flat. I did not want to spoil their holiday so soon. But the spring work is not rushing too fast!" Soon after she wrote this letter, Sarah was taken to the hospital in Kelowna, where she died on 20 April 1919. Fortunately, Lucy and Esther received word that she was ill and appear to have returned from the coast in time to be with their mother in the hospital at the end.

Sarah Craig's dream of finding a better life in a better place never died. She clung to that dream through the births of four-teen children and the deaths of four of these as infants or toddlers, through the early death of her husband at age fifty-one, and through the shattering loss of her eldest daughter, Alice. Having spent much of her life "running away" from one home in search of another, she finally found peace and happiness in the beautiful Okanagan Valley. Certainly, her dream of living in a utopian com-munity remained unfulfilled. Yet her account of her journeys west-ward in search of a better life offer a window on the experience of a determined, self-aware woman whose life spanned some of the most significant years in Canadian history. By the end of her life, she had seen Confederation and the opening up of the Canadian west. She had witnessed the first developments of modern medical knowledge and methods of research, was living in a home with indoor plumbing and a telephone, and had exercised her right to vote, as part of the first generation of Canadian women to do so.

Grounded in her love for her family, Sarah's preoccupations always radiated outward from the domestic sphere to develop-ments in the wider world. Her accounts of her search for her own version of Eden cast new light on the lives and aspirations of rural women like her. It was not only those of the middle and upper classes who dreamed of radical change, of creating a more equal society revolutionized by new ideas and new ways of living. The poor dreamed these dreams as well – and none so eloquently as Sarah Jameson Craig.

Afterword

Sarah Jameson Craig was my great-grandmother. Although I knew about her writings as a child and watched as my grandmother – Sarah's youngest child, Florence – typed them up on her tiny Underwood typewriter, I disliked my grandmother so intensely that I resisted reading them for years. I felt that Grandma was always critical of me, and one of my earliest memories is of feeling ashamed at her rebuke for something I had said or done. By the time I had grown up enough to move past my resentments, Florence had died at the advanced age of ninety-six and was not around to answer any of my questions.

I was over thirty by the time I sat down and read the memoir that my grandmother had typed up. When I finally did, it was a revelation. I was immediately struck by the force of Sarah's voice, by her passion and eloquence. I was also shocked at how critical she often was of Florence, who apparently had a propensity for daydreaming and getting lost in a book – just like me and, ironically, just like Sarah herself in the days before she set off along that lonely road to St Andrews at fourteen. For the first time I understood what it might have been like for Florence to grow up with this mother, who was fiercely intelligent, restless, torn between love for her family and her longing to find a better place, and perhaps always comparing her other daughters to her dear lost Alice. This was a mother who loved Florence deeply and yet could write in her diary about Florence's ineptitude at housework: "what a *child* she is, to be raising a family, & *thinking* she is making a home!" (Later diaries, 6 September 1916). Florence inherited that critical eye and sharp tongue; I had experienced it myself, but now I could understand why.

When I looked further at the materials that had been passed down in the family, I discovered the early diaries: a stack of tiny household notebooks, frayed at the edges, filled with cramped writing in pencil, scribbled by someone clearly desperate to record her thoughts on any bit of paper that she could get her hands on. I also discovered someone who, like me, was from an early age determined to be a writer. The account that first drew me to her was that tale of how she ran away from home, intent on heading off to become a famous writer. What courage! What foolishness! Even at that age she was not content to be restricted to domestic life, but was itching to move forward into the wider world and make her mark on it. How sad that she lived in a time and a place that offered so little to women, especially to women of intelligence. What a waste of her talents.

How lucky I am, with my education and my choices.

Sarah's descendants prospered in various ways, but none of them got rich in the west. Almost all of her surviving children lived into their eighties and nineties. Among the grandchildren, most eventually migrated down to British Columbia's Lower Mainland seeking better job opportunities. Two of the men (my uncles) served in World War II; the women all married and raised children. But poverty was never far away, and it continued to take its toll on the educational opportunities for all. Shell-shocked in World War I, Florence's husband, Edgar, returned from the Front never really able to work again. My mother, Florence's youngest daughter, was raised in poverty; she worked and scrimped and saved to put herself through Normal School to earn her teaching certificate. She was the only one of her generation to attain this level of education.

And I am the only one in my family to have any university degree.

I know now that I am connected to Sarah Jameson Craig in ways I had never imagined. She is the source of my love of writing and my thirst for intellectual engagement. But she is also the source of my grandmother's and even my mother's critical judgments — judgments that were often hurtful. Because I can now trace that thread back through the generations and can see where it came from, I can understand them both much better.

Soon after I first read Sarah's memoir, I travelled to southwestern New Brunswick to look for the imprints of her obscure life. I wanted to find that rebellious girl who had launched herself from home on that winter day long ago. I wanted to walk the road that she had walked. I found the road but little else. In fact, that part of New Brunswick is less populated now than it was in the 1800s.

I set off in my rental car to look for the neighbourhood where Sarah grew up, a place that her parents called Pleasant Ridge. Of course, it's not on the map. Neither is Lakeside, the property that Joel and his mother owned, and where Sarah and Joel built their little shack when the first house burned down. Past the turnoff for Rollingdam, there is a sign for Whittier Ridge Road, and I turned onto a gravel road that looked more like a washed-out stream bed. But it brought me out on top of a mountain, with a view to the west, north, and east. This was Whittier's Ridge, although there were no "ignorant gossiping scandalmongers" to be seen. There were only the small cries of birds and the wind whishing over the stony heath and ruffling the ankle-deep carpet of wild strawberry plants at my feet. There was also the panoramic view of the Digdeguash mountains that Sarah had described in her "Blueberrying Story."

Driving east on the 770, I soon emerged from the woods into a watery marshland where a brook flowed under the road and a vast wetland stretched away on both sides. A little further on, I found Clarence Road, but if there ever was a village called Clarence, it's long gone; all I found were a few houses, empty fields, and a derelict cabin.

I drove back to the marsh, a wondrous place of water and light, and stopped the car. A boy with a fishing rod was standing in the middle of the road. He had just caught a long black eel, which was twisting and gyrating on its hook. I got out and walked toward him. He was maybe twelve.

"What's the name of this stream, the one that runs under the road?" I asked.

"Craig's Brook," he said. "Comes outa Craig's Lake, back of the trees there." He pointed.

My heart started thumping. "Craig's Lake? How do I get there from here?"

He pointed eastward. "Down there about a mile or so ya see a road comin off to yer left. Take you to Craig's Lake."

I drove east, watching carefully, until I saw a pole with a yellow and black square marking a tiny gravel road. I steered the car in and crept along it, sandwiched between two walls of leafy trees. It wasn't long before I reached a cottage built right on the water's edge. Beyond it stretched a calm, shallow lake, its water streaked with rushes. I got out and breathed in the hot fragrance of Balm of Gilead trees.

I'm almost certain that this was the property where Sarah and Joel lived, the place that Joel called Lakeside and about which he wrote a sequence of poems he called "Lakeside Echoes." Somewhere, if I looked and dug, I might find the blackened remnants of that one-room cabin that burned to the ground in 1865, taking with it their colony dreams. And somewhere up the hill, perhaps deep in the shadows, long forgotten, I might find Sarah's "little flower garden," the place where five of her children lie buried.

I drove back to the spot where the road to St Andrews forks off and got out. Standing there in the hot sun, in my jeans, with the wind ruffling my short hair, I wished I could tell Sarah how the future she wished for so fervently had turned out. I wished that I could pass that knowledge back to her, as she had passed her experiences forward to me.

I gazed at that road, the one that still dips downward into the woods. I could almost see her, striding along in the sunshine, ablaze with determination and hope. I thought, What if she walked out of the past right now, right here, and we met on this deserted road? What would we say to each other?

But that shimmer I saw ahead of me was only the waves of heat rising from the pavement.

The Siblings and Children
of Sarah Jameson Craig

Sarah Jameson's Siblings: The Children of Charles Jameson and Alice Woodin Jameson

Albert	born 15 July 1834; died 3 June 1863
Isaac	born 17 April 1836; died 11 October 1917
Sarah	born 10 June 1840; died 20 April 1919
George W.	born 30 June 1842
Henry	born 30 March 1844
Martha	born 15 February 1846
John Howard	born 9 June 1848
William Arthur	born 16 November 1851
Charles Edwin	born 12 January 1854

Four other children died in infancy.

The Children of Sarah Jameson Craig and Joel Bonney Craig

James Albert	born 10 November 1862; died 6 March 6 1863
Albert Jameson	born 2 January 1864; died 6 April 1936
Frank Ernest Freeman	born 30 August 1865; died 18 December 1906

Martha Alice	born 26 June 1867; died 18 April 1893
David James Alexander	born 26 July 1869; died 31 March 1874
Clara Matilda	born 18 December 1870; died 31 March 1874
Joel Bonney	born 24 June 1873; died 13 January 1940
Charles Henry	born 9 June 1875; died 4 August 1966
Lucy Emma	born 5 April 1877; died 12 April 1962
William Rupert	born 26 August 1878; died 16 April 1968
Benjamin	born 25 November 1880; died 25 December 1880
Esther Victoria	born 15 March 1882; died October 1978
Sarah Florence Myrtle	born 13 April 1884; died 7 May 1980

Notes

Introduction

1 McCarthy, "Pocketful of Days," 275.

2 Kagle and Gramegna, "Rewriting Her Life," 39–41.

3 Ibid., 41.

4 Ibid.

5 Morse, *Yankee Communes*, 9.

6 Kesten, *Utopian Episodes*, 268.

7 Noel, *Canada Dry*, 10–12.

8 Whorton, "Patient, Heal Thyself," 56.

9 Ibid., 58.

10 Ibid., 57.

11 Ibid., 58.

12 Smith, *Revivalism and Social Reform*, 141–7.

13 Numbers, *Prophetess of Health*, for Ellen White; Morse, *Yankee Communes*, 13–41 for Mother Ann Lee and 83–112 for George Rapp.

14 Kesten, *Utopian Episodes*, discusses each of these communities.

Chapter One

1 Acheson, "New Brunswick Agriculture."

2 Rees, *St. Andrews and the Islands*, viii.

3 Jameson, *Jamesons in America*, 281.

4 Ibid., 282.

5 Ibid.

6 Stern, *Heads and Headlines*, xii–xiii, 32–3.

7 Cayleff, *Wash and Be Healed*, 15.

8 Ibid., 14.

9 Ibid., 15.

10 Legan, "Hydropathy in America," 277.

11 Kesselman, "'Freedom Suit,'" 497.

12 Cayleff, *Wash and Be Healed*, 6–8.

13 Donegan, *Hydropathic Highway*, 10–11.

14 Ibid., 27–34; Numbers, "Do-it-yourself," 62.

15 Cayleff, *Wash and Be Healed*, 23.

16 Ibid., citing R.T. Claridge, *Hydropathy; or, The Cold Water Cure, as Practised by Vincent Priessnitz* (1842).

17 Cayleff, *Wash and Be Healed*, 38.

18 Ibid.

19 Ibid.

20 Whorton, "Patient, Heal Thyself," 59.

21 Donegan, *Hydropathic Highway*, 186.

22 Ibid.

23 Warner, *Therapeutic Perspective*, 277–82; Fuller, *Alternative Medicine*, 13.

24 Cayleff, *Wash and Be Healed*, 24.

25 "Processes of Water-Cure," *Water-Cure Journal* 1, no. 1 (Dec. 1845): 17–21; "Notes on Water-Cure," *Water-Cure Journal* 1, no. 2 (Jan. 1846): 33–7.

26 *Water-Cure Journal* 8, no. 1 (July 1849): 3–7.

27 Nissenbaum, *Sex, Diet and Debility*, 149.

28 Cayleff, *Wash and Be Healed*, 25.

29 Ditzion, *Marriage, Morals, and Sex*, 328.

30 Cayleff, *Wash and Be Healed*, 49–62.

31 Donegan, *Hydropathic Highway*, 87.

32 Ibid., 193.

33 Cayleff, *Wash and Be Healed*, 66–73.

34 Nichols, "Woman the Physician," *Water-Cure Journal* 12, no. 4 (Oct. 1851): 74.

35 Cayleff, *Wash and Be Healed*, 68–73.

36 Gleason, "Woman's Dress" (Feb. 1851 and Sept. 1851).

37 Gleason, "Woman's Dress" (Feb. 1851), 30; *Water-Cure Journal* 12, no. 4 (Oct. 1851): 74, 96.

38 Kunzle, *Fashion and Fetishism*, 164–72.

39 Summers, *Bound to Please*, 52–5.

40 Donegan, *Hydropathic Highway*, 101.

41 Ibid., 152–3.

42 Severa, *Dressed for the Photographer*, 87.

43 Ibid., 239.

44 Curtis, "'We'll fight for nature-light,'" 113.

45 Ibid.

46 Severa, *Dressed for the Photographer*, 88.

47 Donegan, *Hydropathic Highway*, 137.

48 Hasbrouck, "'Principle' of Dress Reform."

49 Severa, *Dressed for the Photographer*, 88.

50 Ibid.; Cunningham, *Reforming Women's Fashion*, 56–7; Fischer, *Pantaloons and Power*, 106–9.

51 *Water-Cure Journal* 34, no. 4 (Oct. 1862): 89.

52 Quoted in Donegan, *Hydropathic Highway*, 156.

53 Severa, *Dressed for the Photographer*, 88.

54 Donegan, *Hydropathic Highway*, 156.

55 Curtis, "'We'll fight for nature-light,'" 114.

56 *Sibyl* 1 (1859): 36; quoted in Kesselman, "'Freedom Suit,'" 504.

57 Summers, *Bound to Please*, 111.

58 Ibid., 115.

59 *Water-Cure Journal* 7, no. 1 (Jan. 1849): 8–11.

60 Gleason, "Woman's Dress" (Feb. 1851), 31.

61 *Tokology: A Book for Every Woman* (1883), 31; quoted in Summers, *Bound to Please*, 52.

62 Summers, *Bound to Please*, 49.

63 Ibid., 48–54.

64 A handwritten copy of these pledges survives in the papers of descendants of Adam Seed, who was one of these UPRA members. It was donated to the Charlotte County Archives, St Andrews, NB, in 2000.

65 *Herald of Health* 4, no. 2 (Aug. 1864): 80.

66 Donegan, *Hydropathic Highway*, 20–1.

67 Trall, *Hydropathic Encyclopedia*, 2: 162–4.

68 Donegan, *Hydropathic Highway*, 173–4.

69 Ibid., 174.

Chapter Two

1 *Herald of Health* 3, no. 1 (Jan. 1864): 11.

2 Donegan, *Hydropathic Highway*, 98.

3 Kesten, *Utopian Episodes*, 93–112.

4 Cayleff, *Wash and Be Healed*, 29.

5 *Herald of Health* 3, no. 1 (Jan. 1864): 11.

6 *Herald of Health*, 4, no. 2 (Aug. 1864): 57.

7 Ibid.

8 Ibid.

9 Cayleff, *Wash and Be Healed*, 136–58.

10 *Herald of Health* 6, no. 5 (Nov. 1865): 158.

Chapter Three

1 Swedlund and Donta, "Scarlet Fever Epidemics," 159.
2 Ibid.
3 PubMedHealth, "Scarlet Fever."
4 Swedlund and Donta, "Scarlet Fever Epidemics," 159.
5 Ibid., 171.
6 Munde, *Hydriatic Treatment of Scarlet Fever*, 15.
7 *Herald of Health* 4, no. 2 (Aug. 1864): 56.
8 Noyes, *Free Love in Utopia*, xix.
9 Ibid.
10 Ibid., xx–xxi.
11 Tillotson, *History ov the First Thirty-Five Years*, 14.
12 Purdy, *American Dress Reform Movement*, 22–5.
13 Kesselman, "'Freedom Suit,'" 502–6.
14 Quoted in Kesselman, "'Freedom Suit,'" 500.
15 Ibid., 506.

Chapter Four

1 *Founding of Vineland*.
2 Women's Project of New Jersey, *Past and Promise*, 138.
3 *Founding of Vineland*.
4 Ibid.
5 Ibid.
6 Tillotson, *History ov the First Thirty-Five Years*, 14.
7 Women's Project of New Jersey, *Past and Promise*, 198.
8 Dineen, "Vineland's Mary Tillotson."
9 Tillotson, *History ov the First Thirty-Five Years*, 78–81.
10 Women's Project of New Jersey, *Past and Promise*, 138.

11 Friends of Historic Vineland, "Historic Characters."

12 "Dress Reformer Married at 80."

13 Women's Project of New Jersey, *Past and Promise*, 139.

14 Friends of Historic Vineland, "Historic Characters."

15 "Miss Fowler's Trousseau."

16 Tillotson's books are *History ov the First Thirty-Five Years of the Science Costume Movement in the United States of America* (1885), *Progress vs Fashion* (1874), *Woman's Way Out* (1876), and *Love and Transition* (1878).

17 Women's Project of New Jersey, *Past and Promise*, 198–9.

18 *Water-Cure Journal* 1, no. 3 (Jan. 1845): 38.

19 Email from Tonse M.K. Raju, MD, DCH, on Caduceus-l (History of Medicine listserv), 12 March 2013.

20 Trall, *Hydropathic Encyclopedia*, 2: 170–1.

21 Buss, *Mapping Our Selves*, 43–4.

22 *Wikipedia*, "Demographics of Saskatchewan."

23 "Dramatic advertising campaigns promoted the benefits of prairie living. Potential immigrants read leaflets information [*sic*] painted Canada as a veritable garden of Eden, and downplayed the need for agricultural expertise." *Wikipedia*, "History of Saskatchewan."

24 Jameson, *Jamesons in America*, 253–4, 255.

25 Ibid., 281–2.

26 Rouleau and District History Book Committee, *Rouleau and District History*, 26.

27 Ibid., 2.

28 Ibid., 1–2.

29 Quoted ibid., 2.

30 Rouleau Historical Committee, *Record of Activities*, 7.

31 Quoted in Cunningham, *Reforming Women's Fashion*, 218.

32 Fischer, *Pantaloons and Power*, 171–2.

33 Cunningham, *Reforming Women's Fashion*, 56–7.
34 Ibid., 135–52.
35 Waiser, *Saskatchewan*, 102.

Chapter Five

1 Wink, *She Left Nothing in Particular*, 15.
2 Simpson, *Kelowna Story*, 30–44.
3 Ibid., 52.
4 Ibid., 59–61.
5 Ibid., 77–9.
6 Ibid., 82.
7 Ibid.
8 Ibid., 87–8.
9 Wink, *She Left Nothing in Particular*, 8–16.

Bibliography

Primary Sources

Craig, Sarah Jameson. Memoir ("History"), early diaries (1 Jan. 1865–27 Aug. 1889), and later diaries (16 Aug. 1902–24 March 1919). Charlotte County Archives, St Andrews, New Brunswick.

Secondary Sources

Acheson, T.W. "New Brunswick Agriculture at the End of the Colonial Era: A Reassessment." *Acadiensis* 22, no. 2 (Spring 1993): 5–26.
Bunkers, Suzanne L., and Cynthia A. Huff, eds. *Inscribing the Daily: Critical Essays on Women's Diaries*. Amherst: University of Massachusetts Press, 1996.
Buss, Helen M. *Mapping Our Selves: Canadian Women's Autobiography*. Montreal: McGill- Queen's University Press, 1993.
Carson, Gerald. "Bloomers and Bread Crumbs." *New York History* 38 (Jan. 1957): 295–6.
Cayleff, Susan. *Wash and Be Healed: The Water-Cure Movement and Women's Health*. Philadelphia: Temple University Press, 1987.

Cunningham, Patricia A. *Reforming Women's Fashion, 1850–1920*. Kent, Ohio, and London: Kent State University Press, 2003.

Curtis, Jennifer. "'We'll fight for nature-light, truth-light and sunlight, against a world in swaddling clothes': Reconsidering the Aesthetic Dress Movement and Dress Reform in Nineteenth Century America." *Past Imperfect* 13 (2007): 108–33.

Davies, John D. *Phrenology: Fad and Science*. New Haven: Archon Books, 1955.

Dineen, Caitlin. "Vineland's Mary Tillotson Was Once Jailed for Wearing Pants." *Press of Atlantic City*, 23 March 2012. http://www.pressofatlanticcity.com/features/f4/vineland-s-mary-tillotson-was-once-jailed-for-wearing-pants/article_58eb07d2-752a-11e1-9686-001871e3ce6c.html.

Ditzion, Sidney. *Marriage, Morals, and Sex in America: A History of Ideas*. New York: W.W. Norton & Co., 1978.

Donegan, Jane. *Hydropathic Highway to Health: Women and Water-Cure in Antebellum America*. New York: Greenwood Press, 1986.

"Dress Reformer Married at 80." *Boston Evening Transcript*, 1 June 1904. http://news.google.com/newspapers?nid=2249&dat=19040601&id=KB80AAAAIBAJ&sjid=JuEIAAAAIBAJ&pg=5648,30033.

Fischer, Gayle V. *Pantaloons and Power: A Nineteenth-Century Dress Reform in the United States*. Kent, Ohio, and London: Kent State University Press, 2001.

The Founding of Vineland. http://westjersey.org/vland.htm.

Friends of Historic Vineland. "Historic Characters." http://www.friendsofvineland.org/his_char2.htm.

Fuller, Robert C. *Alternative Medicine and American Religious Life*. New York and Oxford: Oxford University Press, 1989.

Gleason, Rachel Brooks. "Woman's Dress." *Water-Cure Journal* 11, no. 2 (Feb. 1851): 30–2.

– "Woman's Dress." *Water-Cure Journal* 12, no. 3 (Sept. 1851): 58–9.

Hasbrouck, Lydia Sayer. "The 'Principle' of Dress Reform." *Sibyl* 1 (15 Jan. 1857): 108.

Herald of Health and Journal of Physical Culture (New-York) 3–6 (1864–65).

Jameson, E.O., ed. *The Jamesons in America.* Boston: Rumford Press, 1901.

Kagle, Steven E., and Lorenza Gramegna. "Rewriting Her Life: Fictionalization and the Use of Fictional Models in Early American Women's Diaries." In *Inscribing the Daily: Critical Essays on Women's Diaries,* ed. Suzanne Bunkers and Cynthia Huff, 38–55. Amherst: University of Massachusetts Press, 1996.

Kesselman, Amy. "The 'Freedom Suit': Feminism and Dress Reform in the United States, 1848–1875." *Gender and Society* 5, no. 4 (Dec. 1991): 495–510.

Kesten, Seymour R. *Utopian Episodes.* Syracuse: Syracuse University Press, 1993.

Kunzle, David. *Fashion and Fetishism: A Social History of the Corset, Tight-lacing and Other Forms of Body-Sculpture in the West.* Totowa, NJ: Rowman and Littlefield, 1982.

Legan, Marshall Scott. "Hydropathy in America: A Nineteenth Century Panacea." *Bulletin of the History of Medicine* 45 (1971): 267–80.

McCarthy, Molly. "A Pocketful of Days: Pocket Diaries and Daily Record Keeping among Nineteenth-Century New England Women." *New England Quarterly* 73, no. 2 (June 2000): 274–96.

"Miss Fowler's Trousseau." *Brookfield Courier,* 3 Aug. 1904. http://fulton history.com/Newspaper4/Brookfield%20NY%20Courier/Brookfield %20NY%20Courier%201904%20-%201906%20grayscale.pdf/Brook field%20NY%20Courier%201904%20-%201906%20grayscale%20- %200122.pdf.

Morse, Flo. *Yankee Communes: Another American Way.* New York:
    Harcourt, Brace, Jovanovich, 1971.

Munde, Charles. *Hydriatic Treatment of Scarlet Fever in Its Different
    Forms.* New York: William Radde, 1857. Available from Project
    Gutenberg.

New York History: The Oneida Community. http://www.nyhistory.com/
    central/oneida.htm.

Nichols, Mary Gove. "Woman the Physician." *Water-Cure Journal* 12,
    no. 4 (Oct. 1851): 73–5.

Nissenbaum, Stephen. *Sex, Diet and Debility in Jacksonian America.*
    Westport: Greenwood Press, 1980.

Noel, Jan. *Canada Dry: Temperance Crusades before Confederation.*
    Toronto: University of Toronto Press, 1995.

Noyes, George Wallingford. *Free Love in Utopia: John Humphrey Noyes
    and the Origin of the Oneida Community.* Ed. Lawrence Foster. Urbana
    and Chicago: University of Illinois Press, 2001.

Numbers, Ronald. "Do-it-yourself the Sectarian Way." In *Medicine
    without Doctors: Home Health Care in American History*, ed. Guenter
    B. Risse, Ronald Numbers, and Judith Leavitt, 49–72. New York:
    Science History Publications, 1977.

– *Prophetess of Health: A Study of Ellen G. White.* Knoxville: University
    of Tennessee Press, 1992.

PubMedHealth. "Scarlet Fever." http://www.ncbi.nlm.nih.gov/pubmed
    health/PMH0001969/.

Purdy, Jane Beryl. "The American Dress Reform Movement of the
    Nineteenth Century." MSc dissertation, Cornell University, 1959.

Rees, Ronald. *St. Andrews and the Islands.* Halifax: Nimbus Publishing,
    1995.

Rouleau and District History Book Committee. *Rouleau and District
    History 1894–1994.* Rouleau, 1995.

Rouleau Historical Committee. *A Record of Activities and Reminiscences of Rouleau and District.* Regina, 1971.

Severa, Joan. *Dressed for the Photographer: Ordinary Americans and Fashion, 1840–1900.* Kent, Ohio: Kent State University Press, 1995.

Sibyl (Middletown, NY) 1 (1857–59).

Simpson, Sharron J. *The Kelowna Story: An Okanagan History.* Madeira Park, BC: Harbour Publishing, 2011.

Smith, Timothy L. *Revivalism and Social Reform in Mid-Nineteenth-Century America.* New York: Abingdon Press, 1957.

Stern, Madeleine B. *Heads and Headlines: The Phrenological Fowlers.* Norman: University of Oklahoma Press, 1971.

Summers, Leigh. *Bound to Please: A History of the Victorian Corset.* Oxford and New York: Berg, 2001.

Swedlund, Alan C., and Alison K. Donta. "Scarlet Fever Epidemics of the Nineteenth Century: A Case of Evolved Pathogenic Virulence?" In *Human Biologists in the Archives: Demography, Health, Nutrition and Genetics in Historical Populations,* ed. D. Ann Herring and Alan C. Swedlund, 159–77. Cambrige: Cambridge University Press, 2003.

Tillotson, Mary E. *History* ov [sic] *the First Thirty-Five Years of the Science Costume Movement in the United States of America.* Vineland, NJ: Weekly Independent Book & Job Office, 1885.

Trall, Russell Thatcher. *The Hydropathic Encyclopedia.* 2 vols. New York: Fowler & Wells, 1851.

Waiser, Bill. *Saskatchewan: A New History.* Calgary: Fifth House Publishers, 2005.

Warner, John Harley. *The Therapeutic Perspective: Medical Practice, Knowledge, and Identity in America, 1820–1885.* Cambridge: Harvard University Press, 1986.

Water-Cure Journal (New-York) 1–34 (1845–62).

Whorton, James C. "Patient, Heal Thyself: Popular Health Reform

Movements as Unorthodox Medicine". In *Other Healers: Unorthodox Medicine in America*, ed. Norman Gevitz, 52–81. Baltimore and London: Johns Hopkins University Press, 1988.

Wikipedia. "Demographics of Saskatchewan." http://en.wikipedia.org/wiki/Demographics_of_Saskatchewan.

– "History of Saskatchewan: Immigration and Settlement Era." http://en.wikipedia.org/wiki/History_of_Saskatchewan#Immigration_and_settlement_era.

Wink, Amy. *She Left Nothing in Particular: The Autobiographical Legacy of Nineteenth-Century Women's Diaries.* Knoxville: University of Tennessee Press, 2001.

Women's Project of New Jersey. *Past and Promise: Lives of New Jersey Women.* Metuchen, NJ, and London: The Scarecrow Press, 1990.

Index